D1613987

Unknown Quantity

Paul Virilio **Unknown Quantity**

 **Thames & Hudson**

Fondation Cartier pour l'art contemporain

In collaboration with AFP and Ina

Contents

Foreword

Paul Virilio

"Contemporary civilization differs in one particularly distinctive feature from those which preceded it: *speed*. The change has come about within a generation," noted the historian Marc Bloch, writing in the nineteen-thirties.

This situation brings in its wake a second feature: the *accident*. The progressive spread of catastrophic events do not just affect current reality, but produce anxiety and anguish for coming generations.

Daily life is becoming a kaleidoscope of incidents and accidents, catastrophes and cataclysms, in which we are endlessly running up against the unexpected, which occurs out of the blue, so to speak. In a shattered mirror, we must then learn to discern what is impending more and more often—but above all more and more quickly, those events coming upon us inopportunely, if not indeed simultaneously.

Faced with an accelerated temporality which affects mores and Art as much as it does international politics, there is one particularly urgent necessity: to expose and to exhibit the *Time accident*.

Turning around the threat of the unexpected in this way, surprise becomes a subject for research and major risks a subject for exposure and for exhibition, within the framework of instantaneous telecommunications.

As Paul Valéry explained in 1935: "In the past, where novelty was concerned, we had almost always seen only solutions or answers to very old—if not indeed age-old—problems... *The novelty of our present situation consists in the unprecedented nature of the questions themselves, not of the solutions, in the statement of the problems, not the answers to them.* Hence a general impression of powerlessness and incoherence predominates in our minds."[1]

This acknowledgement of powerlessness before the upsurge of unexpected, catastrophic events forces us to reverse the usual trend which exposes us to accidents and inaugurate a new kind of museology and museography: one which consists in exposing or exhibiting the accident—all accidents, from the most commonplace to the most tragic, from natural catastrophes to industrial and scientific disasters, including also the kind that is too often neglected, the happy accident, the stroke of luck, the *coup de foudre* or even the *coup de grâce*!

If today, thanks to television, "what is preserved is reduced to the event-instant, all progress converges on an inescapable problem which is that of perceptions and images."[2]

Apart from the historic September 11 attack and its continuous rebroadcasting on all the world's TV screens, two recent events merit harsh analysis in this connection. On the one hand, the revelation *sixteen years too late* of the damage done by the contamination of Eastern France by Chernobyl, on which subject the officials in the department responsible for raising the alarm in April 1986 declared, "*If something is detected, this is a purely scientific problem.*" And, on the other, the very recent decision of the Caen Memorial Peace Museum to import *an atom bomb*—an H-bomb—as a symbolic object from the United States, emblematic of the balance of terror between East and West.

In this connection, echoing the remarks of the French experts who concealed the damage done by the Chernobyl accident, we might say, "*If we are exhibiting an atom bomb, this is a purely cultural problem,*" throwing the doors wide open to the first Museum of accidents!

If, in fact, *invention is just a way of seeing*, of grasping accidents as signs, as opportunities, it is high time to open up our galleries to the impromptu, to that "indirect production" of science and the techno-sciences that is the disaster, the (industrial or other) catastrophe.

If, according to Aristotle, "the accident reveals the substance," the invention of the substance is also the invention of the "accident." Seen this way, the shipwreck is indeed the "futuristic" invention of the ship, the air crash the invention of the supersonic plane, and the Chernobyl meltdown, the invention of the nuclear power station.

Let us take a look now at recent history. While the twentieth century was the century of great exploits—the landing on the moon—and great discoveries in physics and chemistry, not to mention computing and genetics, it seems logical, alas, that the twenty-first century will reap the harvest of the concealed production represented by the most varied of disasters, *to the extent, indeed, that their repetition is becoming a clearly identifiable historical phenomenon.*

Let us listen again to what Valéry has to say on this: "*The instrument is tending to disappear from consciousness.* In everyday parlance, we say that its operation has become automatic. What we must deduce from this is the new equation: consciousness now exists only for accidents."[3]

This recognition of a failing leads to a clear, definitive conclusion: "All that becomes capable of recommencement and repetition becomes obscure, falls silent. Function exists only outside of consciousness."[4]

Given that the declared objective of the Industrial Revolution of the eighteenth century was precisely the repetition of standardized objects (machines, tools, vehicles), in other words of the famous *"criminal substances,"* it is logical to observe today that the twentieth century can in fact be said to have swamped us with *mass-produced accidents*, from the Titanic in 1912 to Chernobyl in 1986, not to mention Seveso and the Toulouse chemical plant disaster of 2001…

So the serial reproduction of the most diverse catastrophes has come to accompany the great discoveries, the great technical inventions, like a shadow, and unless we accept the unacceptable, that is to say, accept that the accident is becoming, in its turn, automatic, the urgent need for an "intelligence (i.e., an understanding) of the crisis of intelligence" is making itself felt in these opening years of the twenty-first century—an understanding of which ecology is the clinical symptom, with the development of a philosophy of postindustrial eschatology still lying before us.

Let us now accept Valéry's postulate: if consciousness exists only for accidents and if things now operate only "outside of" consciousness, the loss of consciousness of the accident, and of the major disaster, would amount not just to thoughtlessness, but to madness—the madness of voluntary blindness to the fatal consequences of our actions and inventions (I am thinking in particular of genetic engineering and the biotechnologies). This is a situation which would be akin to the sudden reversal of philosophy into its opposite. It would be akin to the birth of a philanoia—literally: a love of madness. A love of radical mindlessness, in which the insane character of our acts would not only cease to worry us consciously, but would delight and captivate us.

After the *accident of substance*, we would see the fatal emergence of the *accident of knowledge*, of which information technology may well be the sign by the very nature of its undoubted advances, but also by the incommensurable damage it has done.

In fact, if "the accident is the appearance of the quality of something which was masked by another of its qualities,"[5] the invention of industrial accidents in (land, sea or air) transport or of postindustrial accidents in the fields of information technology or genetics, would be the appearance of a quality too long hidden by the little progress "scientific" knowledge has made by comparison with the scale of "spiritual and philosophical" knowledge, a wisdom accumulated throughout the centuries-long history of civilizations.

Thus, the damage done by the lay or religious ideologies that were the doctrines of totalitarian regimes is about to give way to the damage done by *thought technologies* capable, if we are not careful, of ending in madness, in the crazed love of excess, as the suicidal character of some contemporary actions tends to prove, from Auschwitz to the military concept of Mutually Assured Destruction (M.A.D.), not to mention the "unbalance of terror" ushered in by the suicide squads who attacked the World Trade Center in New York in 2001.

Indeed, to use not weapons, not military instruments, but simple vehicles of air transport to destroy buildings, while being prepared to perish in the operation, is to set up *a fatal confusion between the attack and the accident* and to use the "quality" of the deliberate accident to the detriment of the quality of the aeroplane and the "quantity" of innocent lives sacrificed, thus exceeding all limits previously set by religious or philosophical ethics.

The principle of responsibility to future generations requires that we expose accidents now, and the frequency of their industrial and post-industrial repetition.

This is the very point, the avowed aim of the Fondation Cartier exhibition. A pilot project for, or more exactly a prefiguration of, the future Museum of the Accident. This exhibition aims above all to take a stand against the fading ethical and aesthetic points of reference, and the loss of meaning in which we are so often now not really actors, but witnesses or victims.

After the exhibition more than ten years ago on speed organized at Jouy-en-Josas also by the Fondation Cartier pour l'art contemporain, the exhibition *Unknown Quantity* aims to provide a counterpoint to the excesses of all kinds with which the great news media swamp us daily, a museum of horrors, which no one seems to realize always precedes and accompanies the upsurge of even greater disasters.

In fact, as one witness to the rise of nihilism in Europe put it, "The most atrocious act becomes easy when the path leading to it has been duly cleared."[6]

By progressive habituation to insensitivity and indifference in the face of the craziest scenes, endlessly repeated by the various "markets of the spectacle" in the name of an alleged *freedom of expression* that has transformed itself into a *liberation of expressionism*—if not indeed an academicism of horror—we are succumbing to the ravages of a *programming of extravagance at any cost* which ends not any longer in meaninglessness, but in the heroicization of terror and terrorism.

Almost as in the nineteenth century, when official art strove in its Salons to glorify the great battles of the past and ended, as we know, in the mass slaughter of Verdun, we look on, dumbfounded, in these early years of the twenty-first century, as efforts are made to promote artistic torture, aesthetic self-mutilation and suicide as an art-form.

It is, ultimately, to escape this "overexposure of the public to horror" that the Fondation Cartier has adopted the principle of a critical distance from excesses of whatever kind among recent events.

With its aim of raising the issue of the unexpected and the lack of concern at major risks, the event which opens in Paris around the time of the first anniversary of the World Trade Center attack in New York aims to be a homage to discernment, to (philosophical or scientific) preventive understanding in troubled times—times when threats of a worst-case *philanoia*[7] are rife, threats of a love of madness taking as its motto the drunken driver's words to his passenger: *"I'm an accident looking for somewhere to happen."*

Notes

1. Paul Valéry, "La crise de l'intelligence", *Œuvres Complètes*, I (Paris: La Pléiade, 1957).

2. Paul Valéry, *Cahiers*, II, (Paris: La Pléiade, 1960), p. 851.

3. *Op. cit.*, p. 212.

4. *Ibid.*

5. *Op. cit.*, p. 229.

6. Hermann Rauschning, *The Revolution of Nihilism: Warning to the West* (New York: Longmans, Green and Co./Alliance Book Corporation, 1939).

7. Paul Virilio, *Ground Zero* (London: Verso, 2002).

Text translated from French by Chris Turner

Articulation disarticulated: Deconstruction

Following pages:
September 21, 1999, Wufeng, Taiwan
Hotel toppled by Taiwan's strongest earthquake of the past century:
at least 1,546 people killed and 3,841 injured

The cubism of an anti-seismic success

January 24, 1995, Kobe, Japan
Caved-in street after the heavy earthquake that struck Kobe
on January 17th, 1995: more than 5,000 people killed
© AFP/Yoshikuzu Tsuno

The ground falls away

September 21, 1999, Wufeng, Taiwan
Residential building tilting precariously after an earthquake
measuring 8.1 on the Richter scale:
at least 1,546 people killed and 3,841 injured
© AFP/Johnson Liu

November 14, 1999, Duzce, Turkey
Collapsed building after an earthquake measuring 7.2 on the Richter scale,
the second major quake in the region within three months:
at least 347 people killed and almost 3,000 injured
© AFP/Manoocher Deghati

Earthquake
Mosaic of the apse of
Monreale's cathedral, Sicily, Italy,
13th century (detail)
© G. Dagli Orti, Paris

"Deluded philosophers who cry, 'All is well,'
Hasten, contemplate these frightful ruins,
This wreck, these shreds, these wretched ashes of the dead;
These women and children heaped on one another,
These scattered members under broken marble."

Voltaire, *Poem on the Disaster of Lisbon*, 1756

November 1, 1755, Lisbon, Portugal
Earthquake
Lithograph from the German School, 1755
© Bridgeman Giraudon

9

1906, San Francisco, United States
Rift in the road after
the San Francisco earthquake
© Corbis

April 29, 1906, San Francisco, United States
The earthquake of 1906
Engraving by Achille Beltrame
published in *La Domenica Del Corriere*
© G. Dagli Orti, Paris

Colombus, Ohio, United States
Collapsed road in West Broad Street
© Bettmann/Corbis

September 23, 2001, Toulouse, France
Crater caused by the explosion at the AZF factory: 29 people killed,
more than 1000 injured and much damage in Toulouse
© AFP

1

Barringer Crater, Winslow, Arizona, United States
Crater caused by the impact of a meteorite 50,000 years ago:
800 metres in width and 200 meters in depth
© Cosmos/Science Photo Library/David Parker

April 1984
Impact on a satellite's thermal panel of a tiny flake of paint
coming from another spacecraft (image enlarged 100,000 times):
18 impacts per square meter after 50 months in orbit
© Cosmos/Nasa/Science Photo Library

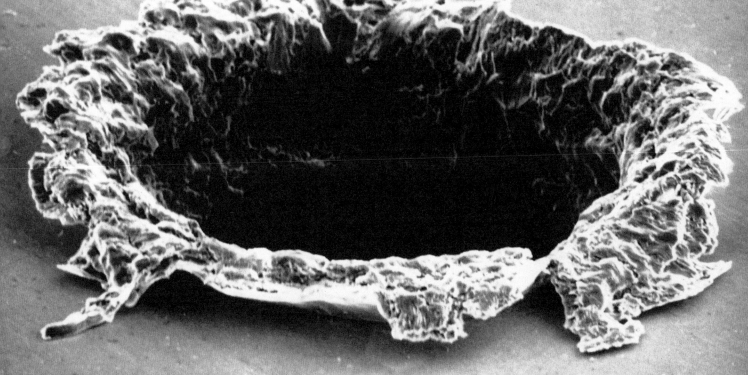

The invention of accidents

Paul Virilio

As both Creation and Fall, the accident is an unconscious work, an *invention* in the classical sense of uncovering that which was hidden—before it emerges into the light of day.

Unlike the **natural** accident, the **man-made** accident is the product of the introduction of a new device or material substance. Whether it be the wreck of the Titanic or the Chernobyl power station explosion—emblematic catastrophes of the last century—the question raised by the accidental event is not so much that of the iceberg looming up in the North Atlantic on a particular night in 1912, or of the nuclear reactor triggering a chain reaction on a particular day in the year 1986, as of the production of the "unsinkable" liner or of the siting of an atomic power station near inhabited areas.

In 1922, for example, when Howard Carter discovered Tutankhamun's sarcophagus in the Valley of the Kings, he literally invented it, but when the Soviet "liquidators" covered the faulty Chernobyl reactor with another kind of "sarcophagus," *they were inventing the major nuclear accident*, and doing so just a few years after the Three Mile Island Accident in the United States.

So, just as Egyptology is a discipline of historical discovery or, in other words, of *archaeological invention*, the analysis of the industrial accident should be perceived as a "logical art" or, more precisely, an **archaeo-technological** invention.

An "*art brut*," in all senses of the term, which we cannot consider only as representing an exception, or examine from the preventative angle of the "precautionary principle" alone, but which we must also see as a major work of the *unconscious spirit of the scientists*, the fruit of Progress and human labour.

We observe however that, though technologies are always in advance of the mentality of the *users*—who need several years to familiarize themselves with a new technology— they are always just as far ahead of the mentality of the *makers*, those engineers who strain their ingenuity to invent devices, to the point where the identification of a *machinic unconscious* by psychoanalysis shows itself to be well-founded, as the *reductio ad absurdum* of the fateful inconsequentiality of scientists where the knowledge of major risks is concerned.

"There is no science of the accident," warned Aristotle long ago. In spite of *cyndinics*, the new science of risk-assessment, there is no *accidentology*, but chance discovery, archaeo-technological invention: to invent the sailing vessel or the steam ship is to *invent the shipwreck*. To invent the train is to *invent the derailment*. To invent the private car is to produce *the motorway pile-up*. To make craft which are heavier than air fly—the aeroplane, but also the dirigible—is to invent the *plane crash*, the air disaster. As for the Challenger space shuttle, its explosion in flight in the same year as the Chernobyl tragedy was the *original accident* of a new device, equivalent to the first shipwreck of the very first sea-going vessel.

Then there is the *indirect invention* of the "crashing" of computer (or other) systems, and the economic disruption of the financial markets with the stock market crash, where suddenly the hidden side of economic science and of the technologies of automatic share-price quotation looms up like the Titanic's iceberg—only this time in Wall Street, Tokyo and London.

So, for Aristotle in his day and for us today, if *the accident reveals the substance*, it is indeed the "*accidens*"—what happens—which is a kind of analysis, a techno-analysis of what "*substat*"—lies beneath—all knowledge.

Once we understand this, then to battle against the harm done by Progress is, first and foremost, to discover the hidden truth of our successes, that accidental—though in no sense apocalyptic—revelation of the *substances incriminées*[1].

Hence the urgent need, on the threshold of the third millennium, for public recognition of this type of innovation which is parasitic upon all technology, an innovation of which the twentieth century repeatedly offered us the most striking examples—as at Bhopal or Seveso, for example, not to mention Toulouse…

At this level, too, *political ecology* can no longer finesse the eschatological dimension of the tragedies caused by the positivistic ideology of Progress.

The *dromologist* or, in other words, the analyst of acceleration phenomena, is being consistent, then, when he takes the view that, if *speed* is responsible for the exponential development of the *man-made accidents* of the twentieth century, it is equally responsible for the greater incidence of *ecological accidents* (in the various cases of environmental pollution), as it is for the *eschatological tragedies* that loom with the recent discoveries relating to the computing of the *genome* and biotechnology[2].

Whereas, in the past, the *local accident* was still precisely situated (*in situ*)—the North Atlantic for the Titanic, for example—the *global accident* no longer is, and its fall-out extends to entire continents. Waiting in the wings is the **integral accident**, which may, some day soon, become our only **habitat**, with the deleterious effects of Progress extending this time not merely to the whole of geophysical space but, most importantly, to a time span of many centuries—not to mention the potentially unprecedented dimension of a "cellular Hiroshima".

If substance is, in fact, *absolute* and *necessary* (to science) and the accident *relative* and *contingent*, we can now equate "substance" with the beginning of knowledge, and the "accident" with *the end* of that philosophical intuition initiated by Aristotle and a few others.

Far from advocating a "millenarian catastrophism" here, it is not a question of taking *a tragic view* of the accident for the purpose of frightening the masses, as the mass media so often do, but only, at last, of taking the accident *seriously*.

Following the example of Freud's work on our relationship to death and its drive, it is now a question of scrupulously studying *our relationship to the end*, to all ends— in other words, to **finitude**.

"Accumulation puts an end to the impression of chance," wrote Sigmund Freud between 1914 and 1915… Since the twentieth century in fact, with the sudden *amassing of tragedies and catastrophes of all kinds*, we have seen confirmation of the collapse of a techno-scientific Progress on which nineteenth-century positivism so prided itself.

Since then, mass production in the spirit of enterprise has literally *industrialized the man-made accident*—whereas that type of accident used to be *artisanal* in character and most often expressed itself discreetly in an age when *natural* accidents, with the exception of wars of extermination, monopolized the cataclysmic dimension.

If we take the area of private motoring, for example, the way the motorway death-toll has come to be accepted as a fact of life is the Freudian proof that the accumulation of traffic accidents largely puts an end to "chance"—and the multiple security systems with which our vehicles are equipped will do nothing to change this fact: in the course of the twentieth century, **accidents became a heavy industry**.

2

But let us come back to a techno-analysis which is revelatory of the "substance" or, in other words, of what lies beneath the technicians' knowledge.

If technologies are always ahead of the mentalities of the personnel responsible for their innovations—as indeed John Berger willingly acknowledges when he writes, *"In any creative work, whether it be an original idea, a painting or a poem, error is always present alongside the skill. But skill is never present alone, there is never any skill or creative talent without error."*[3]—this is because the accident is inseparable from its *velocity of unexpected emergence*, and it is therefore this "virtual velocity" of catastrophic surprise that has to be studied, not just the "actual velocity" of recently invented objects and devices.

Just as we must forearm ourselves (at all costs) with brakes and automatic security systems against the *excess of real speed*, so we must attempt to protect ourselves from the *excess of virtual speed*, from what occurs unexpectedly to "substance"—that is to say, to what lies *beneath* the productive consciousness of the engineer.

This is the "archaeo-technological" discovery or invention referred to above.

In his *Physics*, Aristotle remarks at the outset that it is not Time as such that corrupts and destroys, but the *accidens*—that which happens. It is, then, *passage into Time* or, to put it another way, speed of emergence, which effects the ruin of all things, each "substance" being, in the end, the *victim of the accident of temporal circulation*.

One can easily imagine, then, the damage wrought by the Time accident—the accident that occurs with the instantaneity of the *temporal compression* of data accompanying globalisation—and the unimaginable risks of the synchronization of knowledge.

So, the "imperative of responsibility" of which Hans Jonas speaks, should be based, in the first instance, on the need for a new understanding of *accidental production*— that unconscious industry the "materialist" man of science refuses to face up to, even though the "military-industrial complex" showered us with incidences of the sudden militarization of the sciences throughout the last century, the prime examples being the fateful invention of weapons of mass destruction and of a thermonuclear bomb capable of extinguishing all life on the planet...[4]

In fact, the *visible velocity* of substance—the velocity of a means of transport or the speed of calculation or information—is only ever the emergent part of the iceberg of the—*invisible*—velocity of the **accident**. And this applies both in the realms of road traffic and the circulation of values.

To be convinced of this, one need only observe the most recent stock-exchange crashes, the successive bursting of speculative bubbles on the single market of what is now an interconnected financial system.

Given this state of affairs, catastrophic in very large measure for the very future of humanity, we must necessarily acknowledge the urgent need to make perceptible—if not visible—the speed of the emergence of the accident, of those accidents that plunge history into mourning.

In order to do this, we must attempt *as quickly as possible*—while the vain search goes on for some **black box** that could reveal the parameters of the contemporary catastrophe—to bring out the flagrant character of the disaster specific to new technologies, and to do this by drawing on scientific expertise, of course, but also by way of a philosophical and cultural approach, which may no longer be said to have anything to do with the *publicistic expressionism* of the promoters of technical equipment since, as Malraux once put it, *"Culture is what makes man something other than an accident of the Universe."*

Notes

1. *Substances incriminées* may refer both to substances responsible for some kind of harm in a particular process and, more generally and idiomatically, to "illegal substances", i.e. drugs [Trans.].

2. Let us not forget that it is the intensive use of powerful computers that has facilitated the decoding of the map of the human genome, thus fostering the fateful emergence of the genetic accident.

3. The "Signatures of the Invisible" Conference, organized by CERN, the London Institute and the Gulbenkian Foundation, was held at Lisbon in Autumn 2002 in the presence of John Berger, Maurice Jacob and the author of these lines.

4. One example of scientific inconsequentiality is the announcement on July 13, 2002 that a *synthetic poliomyelitis virus* had been created in laboratory conditions, polio being an illness that is almost totally eradicated today. Speaking on this matter, Robert A. Lamb, the president of the American Society for Virology expressed the fear that terrorists may in the future develop biological weapons of this type.

Text translated from French by Chris Turner

Jan Van Scorel,
The Universal Deluge, 16th century (detail)
© G. Dagli Orti, Paris

Lightning over water (Wim Wenders)…
Lightning Field (Walter de Maria)…

Sea Point, Cape Town, South Africa
Storm at sea
© Getty Images

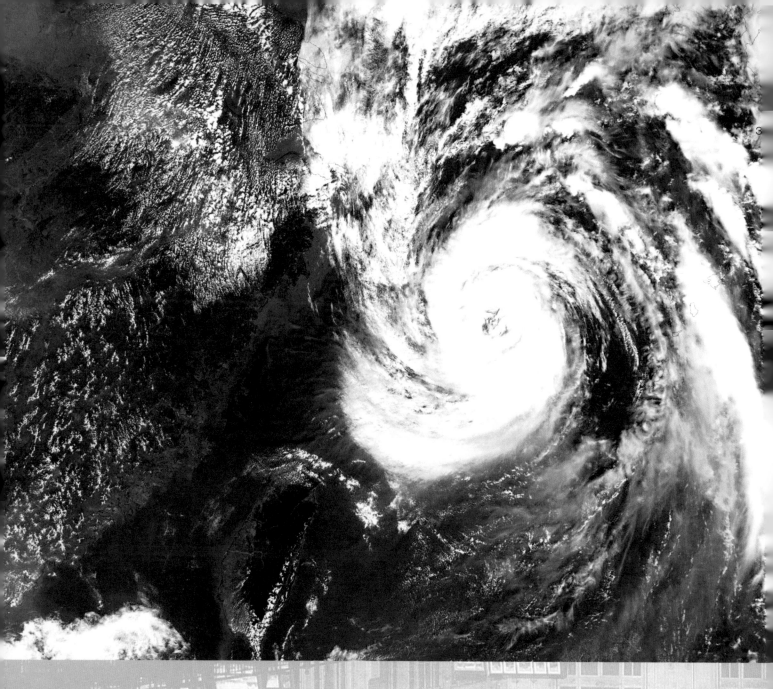

September 14, 2001, China Sea
Satellite image of typhoon Nari in the East China Sea
before it slammed into Taiwan dumping torrential rains
and killing more than 50 people
© AFP/NASA

What is in the gaze of the eye of the cyclone?

Butterfly wing

October 28, 1997, Pacific Ocean
Satellite image showing water vapor in Earth's upper troposphere
(about 10 kilometers above the surface), indicating
the presence of *El Niño*: the warmest equatorial Pacific Ocean water
is displaced toward the east, as shown in the red areas,
causing cyclones and floods
© AFP/NASA

July 15, 1987, Le Grand-Bornand, Haute Savoie, France
Caravan impaled on a tree at the Grand-Bornand camping grounds,
which were destroyed by a torrent of mud on July 14, 1987:
22 people killed and 28 missing
© AFP

René Magritte,
The Song of the Storm, 1937
© G. Dagli Orti, Paris

1910, Paris, France
The Seine floods: view of the interior of the Orsay station
© Roger-Viollet/Branger

1178

3

Above:
1910, Paris, France
The Seine floods: view on the cathedral
of Notre-Dame de Paris
© Roger-Viollet

"No more roads, no riverbanks, no directions;
a flat substance going nowhere,
suspending mankind's development, detaches him
from any rationale, from any utility of places."

Roland Barthes, *Mythologies*, 1970

July 31, 1993, Chesterfield, Missouri, United States
Flooding of Highway 40
©AFP/Peter Newcomb

January 9, 1998, Montreal, Canada
Power lines crushed with the weight of four days accumulated frost in Boucherville,
near Montreal. Some 3 million people without power across Canada
© AFP/Robert Laberge

May 24, 1973, Union City, Oklahoma, United States
One of the violent tornados that devastated
Oklahoma in the spring of 1973
© AFP/NOAA

February 22, 1999, Evolène, Switzerland
Avalanche slamming into the Swiss ski resort of Evolene:
2 people killed and more than 12 missing
© AFP/Fabrice Coffrini/Keystone

July 30, 1908, North Siberia, Russia
Destroyed forest around the point of impact
of the 40,000 ton Tunguska meteorite
© Roger-Viollet

Meteorite or fragment of anti-matter?

The storm as scorched earth policy

December 29, 1999, Nancy, France
Forest destroyed by a violent storm in eastern France on December 25, 1999
© AFP/Franck Fife

The accident thesis

"Progress and catastrophe are the opposite faces of the same coin."

Hannah Arendt

Paul Virilio

Recently, as though the accident had become an *option*, a privilege accorded to chance—to the detriment of the presumption of error or of wilful harm—the "accident thesis" has become a recurrent theme in the mass media, thereby indicating the confusion which is setting in, on the one hand between breakdown and sabotage and, on the other, between the suicide attack and the industrial (or other) accident.

In fact, the unprecedented growth in catastrophes between the beginning of the twentieth century and our own day when, for the first time, there are more "man-made" accidents than "natural" ones, faces each of us with a choice: we must each opt for one version or the other of a current tragic event. Hence this strangely academic term: the accident thesis.

Since the beginning of the last century, breakdowns or failures have progressively become not exactly an unexpected surprise, but rather a subject for theoretical speculation, *a thesis-subject*, allowing the very term "accident" to lose the philosophical definition that had been its own since Aristotle.

Suddenly, the accident is no longer unexpected; it is becoming an – *a priori* scandalous – rumour, in which the presumption of wrongdoing tends to win out over that of involuntary action and, yet, conversely, the quasi-certainty of wilful harm is dissimulated beneath a concern not to provoke panic.

We may note here the guilt immediately ascribed to those who refuse to accept the *official thesis* regarding wrongdoing or accident and who favour a version quite different from that of the established authorities.

Moreover, as soon as the catastrophic event emerges in its "terroristic" dimension, the term employed is no longer that of "thesis", but the police term, the *trail* or *track* of a criminal act.

This semantic uncertainty provides quite a good illustration of the coming confusion between the "true" accident, happening unexpectedly to substance, and the indirect strategy of an act of clear malevolence, but one which rejects the obvious declaration of hostilities as demanded in the past by the rules of classical warfare. *The aim is, of course, to generate fear, but at all costs to avoid the rejection of a terror which is both unspeakable and counterproductive for its anonymous perpetrators* in a society where the screen has become the substitute for the battlefield of the great wars of the past.

The general trend towards the denial of any deliberate attack—the emergent form of a new type of historical denial to rank alongside that of the holocaust—now goes hand in hand with the importance of a country's *brand image*, the image of a nation open to a constantly developing cross-border tourist industry, growing thanks to the low cost of transcontinental transport. Hence the seriousness of the New York attacks, which threw into question not just the United States' status as a sanctuary, but also the rise of the great airline companies and the liberalization of tourist migrations, not to mention the catastrophic impact of the collapse of the Twin Towers on the comprehensive insurance market[1].

From now on, in the face of omnipresent risk, and often even of a major risk for humanity, the question of the *management of fear* becomes once again a prime necessity. To paraphrase an author complicit in this, we might even assert today that, "if knowledge can be represented figuratively as a sphere constantly increasing in volume, the *surface of contact with the unknown is expanding inordinately.*"[2] Replacing the geometric term sphere by the spatio-temporal one dromosphere, we might easily conclude that if the speed of increase of the unknown promotes fear, this fear of the final end of humanity, of which the ecological movement represents a first sign, ought to augment further in the twenty-first century, with a final—and in this case eschatological—movement yet to come, which would garner the dividends of terror.

The sudden questioning of a *substantial warfare*, which was the product of politics, by hyperterrorism, an *accidental warfare* which no longer speaks its name, is also a questioning of politics, and not just traditional party politics. Hence the alternation now, not so much between classic Left and Right as between the political and media spheres, or, in other words, between politics and that power of management (or suggestion) on the part of the news and information media, which are readying themselves to invade the imagination of populations held in thrall by this proliferation of screens, so characteristic of the globalization of "affects"; this sudden synchronization of collective emotions which greatly assists the *administration of fear*.

    To administer fear so as to manage civil peace or, conversely, to administer fear so as to win a civil war—this is the alternative currently characterizing the psychopolitics of nations.

As we can easily see, doubt and worry over the origins of accidents are an integral part of this covert administration of emotions, to the point where, in the very near future the *Ministry of War* might give way to that *Ministry of Fear* that is run by the cinema and the mass media—constituent parts of that *audiovisual continuum* which has now replaced the public space in our daily lives.

Hence this urgent strategic need to preserve uncertainty regarding the origin of any "accident" for as long as possible, since the declared enemy and the official hostilities between old-style states has given way now to the *anonymous attack* and the sabotaging of daily life in the sphere of public transport or business, and in the home.

A convincing example of this transmutation of "political show-business" is provided by the American film *The Sum of All Fears*, sponsored by the U.S. Department of Defense with the direct aid of the CIA and its agent Chase Brandon, who goes so far as to invoke as a watchword for his agency the verse from St. John's gospel: *"And ye shall know the truth, and the truth shall make you free"*[3] (John 8:32).

I n the winter of 2001, the American Ministry of Defense announced the discrete, not to say furtive, creation of the OSI, the *Office of Strategic Influence*. Under the control of the Undersecretary of Defense for Policy, Douglas Feith, this office, a veritable Ministry of Disinformation, was to be responsible for disseminating false news designed to influence a terrorist enemy—itself a somewhat diffuse entity… A *strategy of deception* from which the media of the United States' allies would clearly not be exempt.

Very soon however, as was to be expected, the Defense Secretary, Donald Rumsfeld condemned this project, with its intention to manipulate the public opinion of enemy or allied states. At the end of February, then, the OSI affair seemed to be officially closed. Or was it?

A fine example of an information accident or, in other words, of *media mystification*, aimed at casting doubt on the truth of the facts and in that way creating concern about diffuse threats, where disturbance of the perception of events always works to heighten popular anxiety.

Suicide-attack or *accident*? *Information* or *disinformation*? No one really knows any longer.

In this one example among many others, it remains the *privilege of the accident* (for as long as is necessary) to administer this public fear, which has nothing to do with the private fear of individuals, since the goal pursued is, first and foremost, the *control of emotions* for psycho-political ends.

In the face of this concatenation of media events, each more catastrophic than the rest (the anthrax virus, the threat of a radiological bomb etc.), it is right and proper, then, to enquire into the dramatization that is currently ongoing, since the beginning of the twenty-first century, with the events in New York, Jerusalem and Toulouse, as in Karachi or elsewhere. The prime aim of this dramaturgy: *never to break the chain of emotion engendered by the catastrophic scenes.*

Hence this crescendo towards the end of a media spectacle, a crescendo first introduced by Greek tragedy, at the same time as it was also ushering in Athenian democracy.

For the ancient historian, as for the modern philosopher, the *tragic chorus is the city itself*, where the future is played out, between the threat of a single individual and the *war of each against all*, that stasis from which democracy must protect itself as much as from the solitary tyrant.

With the globalisation of the real time of telecommunications in these early years of the century, the *public stage* of the theatre of origins gives way (and how!) to the *public screen*, where the "acts of the people" are played out—that liturgy in which serial cataclysms and catastrophes have the role of a *deus ex machina* or, alternatively, of the oracle announcing the horrors yet to come and, in this way, denouncing the abomination of the destiny of peoples.

With television, which enables hundreds of millions of people to see the same event at the same moment, we are finally experiencing the same dramaturgical performance as we once did in the theatre. Now, as Arthur Miller explains, "There is no longer any difference between politics and show business. It is the performance that persuades us the candidate is sincere."[4]

To the point where the people's elected representative is barely anything more than a walking, talking audience ratings index! To preserve the illusion at all costs, to preserve the drama being played out before your incredulous eyes—that is the objective of the contemporary mass media of the *era of opinion synchronization*, and all that destroys this collective "harmony" must be implacably censored.

Since September 11, 2001, as we have seen, the media coverage of acts of violence has developed on all fronts. From local delinquency to the global hyper-violence of terrorism, the media hype has been such that no one could escape it for long, and the accumulation of facts of different kinds has gradually produced the impression that *when the World Trade Center collapsed, every form of protection went with it*[5].

This dramatic representation has created a double fear in television viewers, a stereo-anxiety.

To the fear of public insecurity has been added the fear of the images of "audiovisual" insecurity, suddenly throwing domestic terror *into relief*, in such a way as to increase collective anxiety. "We live on the echo, and in this topsy-turvy world the echo arouses the call," observed Karl Kraus[6].

This *mute cry* of the host of the absent, present at the same moment in front of their screens and contemplating the disaster in a state of stupefaction, is not without its consequences. The result of the recent French elections gives fulsome proof of this, since, "It is no longer so much the event as the anaesthesia making it possible and bearable which provides us with explanations."[7]

The sudden stereoscopic casting into relief of the event, be it accident or attack, is indeed, then, the birth of an ultimate form of tragedy—a tragedy not merely audiovisual, but binocular and stereophonic, in which the perspective of the real time of synchronized emotions subjugates minds to this "terrorism of eye-witness evidence," which further reinforces the authority of the media.

Accident or attack? Uncertainty is now the rule, and the mask of the Medusa is forced upon everyone thanks to the helmet of Minerva or, rather, that helmet known as the HMD (head-mounted display), which provides us endlessly with the (mirror) repetition of a horror that fascinates us totally.

On May 6, 1937, in the late afternoon near New York, the dirigible Hindenburg went up in flames over Lakehurst. It was the first great air catastrophe of the twentieth century and it was to leave thirty-four dead. A young journalist reported the event live on radio. His name was Orson Welles, echoing that of the novelist who, thirty years earlier, described the bombing of New York by German dirigibles in his book, *The War in the Air*[8]. In thirty interminable seconds, this flying luxury liner had flamed up like a torch in front of the news cameras and the thousands of onlookers awaiting the Zeppelin's arrival.

Accident or sabotage? Three commissions of enquiry sought to determine the causes of this spectacular tragedy in that politically troubled period… *In very short order, the final communiqué was to favour the accident thesis*, thereby leading to the definitive abandonment of passenger transport in this kind of aircraft.

Here again, without radio and Fox-Movietone newsreels, this major accident would not have had the mythic reverberations it had, being in no way comparable, for example, with the Titanic disaster twenty-five years earlier which left 1,500 dead.

Similarly, without the combined genius of Orson Welles and Herbert George Wells, this event of great moment for the future of relations between the United States and Nazi Germany would not have had its place in history—at the precise moment when, for want of a *War of the Worlds* (also dramatized by Orson Welles), the Second World War was to break out, which would eventually leave the sky aglow over Hiroshima and Nagasaki.

When preparations are being made not merely to re-launch travel by dirigible, but also to bring into operation 500-1,000-seater transatlantic aircraft, we then may ask where the qualitative (if not the quantitative) progress lies in this constant race for greater size.

Air crash or *sabotage*? There will be no end to the asking of this question, unless we eventually come to the view that the fact of wishing to have thousands of passengers fly *at the same moment in one and the same aircraft* is already an accident, or more exactly a sabotaging, of futurological intelligence.

Notes

1. The International Civil Aviation Organization has approved the creation of a world air insurance scheme
   covering risks of war which would fill the gap that would be left if the private insurers were to withdraw partially or wholly
   from this field after the 11 September attacks (*Le Monde*, 18 June 2002).

2. Francesco di Castri.

3. "La CIA au service de Hollywood" (*Le Journal du Dimanche*, 16 June 2002).

4. Arthur Miller, speaking of his book, *On Politics and the Art of Acting* (New York: Viking, 2001).

5. "L'insécurité, programme préféré de la télé" (*Libération*, 28 April 2002).

6. Karl Kraus, *In These Great Times*, p. 77.

7. *Op. cit.*

8. H. G. Wells, *The War in the Air*.

Text translated from French by Chris Turner

January 1992, Amazonia, Brazil
Colourized satellite image showing in red the zones of deforestation;
some of the felling zones measure up to 20 square kilometres
© AFP/ESA

To what desert?

1991, Amazonia, Brazil
Deforestation: 11.3 million hectares of forest
destroyed every year in the world
© AFP/Antonio Scorza

North Dakota, United States
Forest fire
© Corbis/Michael S. Yamashita

June 21, 2002, Phœnix, Arizona, United States.
Infrared satellite image of two forest fires, one a case of arson,
in Arizona; the two fires merged the following day,
destroying more than 410,000 acres of forest and threatening
the town of Show Low.
© AFP/NASA

1906, San Francisco, United States
The fire after the San Francisco earthquake of 1906
© Corbis/Murat

December 16 and 17, 1836, New York, United States
New York fire
Engraving by William James Bennett
© Bridgeman Giraudon

1838, London, United Kingdom
London fire: the Royal Exchange consumed by the flames
Lithograph by John Reeve, 1838
© Bridgeman Giraudon

Joseph Mallord William Turner,
The Burning of the Houses of Lords and Commons, October 16, 1834, 1835
Oil on canvas, 92 x 123.2 cm
© The Cleveland Museum of Art

July 22, 1997, Paris, France
Fire in the Palais de Chaillot, the Museum of French Monuments:
museum collections endangered
© AFP/Jack Guez

August 20, 1997, the Soufrière, Montserrat
View of the lava flow after the eruption of the Soufrière volcano on August 20, 1997
© AFP/Dominique Chomereau-Lamotte

January 26, 2002, Goma, Democratic Republic of Congo
A bulldozer removes lava from Goma town after the eruption of the volcano Mount Nyiragongo:
nearly half a million refugees fleeing towards Rwanda
© AFP/Pedro Ugarte

January 19, 2002, Goma Airport, Democratic Republic of Congo
Waves of lava responsible for the near-total destruction of Goma, second largest city of Congo,
following the eruption of Mount Nyiragongo on January 17, 2002: 500,000 refugees sent fleeing towards Rwanda
© AFP/Marco Longari

June 12, 1991, Clark Air Base, Philippines
Eruption of the volcano Mount Pinatubo sends a cloud of cinders
more than 20 kilometers high
© AFP/Arlan Naeg

Natural accident or nuclear attack?...

August 24, 1968, Mururoa, Tuamotu Islands, Pacific Ocean
Nuclear tests: first explosion of the French hydrogen bomb
© Keystone

…The perception of the accident is always a

accident of perception"

The Museum of accidents

Paul Virilio

A society which rashly privileges the present—real time—to the detriment of both the past and the future, also privileges the accident.

Since, at every moment and most often unexpectedly, everything happens, a civilization that sets immediacy, ubiquity and instantaneity to work brings Accidents and catastrophes on to the scene.

The confirmation of this state of affairs is provided for us by insurance companies, and particularly by the recent Sigma study, carried out for the world's second-largest re-insurance company, Swiss Re.

This recently published study, which each year lists *man-made* disasters (explosions, fires, terrorism etc.) and *natural* catastrophes (floods, earthquakes, storms etc.), takes into account only those disasters causing losses in excess of 35 million dollars.

"For the first time," the Swiss analysts observe, "since the nineteen-nineties, a period when damage due to natural catastrophes predominated over man-made damage, *the trend has reversed, with man-made damage standing at 70%.*"[1]

Proof, if proof were needed, that far from promoting quietude, our industrialized societies throughout the twentieth century have essentially developed disquiet and the major risk, and this is so even if we leave out of account the recent proliferation of weapons of mass destruction… Hence the urgent need to reverse this trend which *consists in exposing us to the most catastrophic accidents* produced by the techno-scientific spirit, and to establish the opposite approach which would consist in exposing or exhibiting the accident as the major enigma of modern Progress.

Although some car companies carry out *more than 400 crash tests annually* in the attempt to improve the safety of their vehicles, this still does not prevent television channels from continually inflicting road-death statistics on us (not to mention the tragedies which see the present repeatedly plunged into mourning). It is certainly high time (alongside the *ecological* approaches that relate to the various ways in which the biosphere is polluted) for the beginnings of an *eschatological* approach to technical progress to emerge—an approach to that finitude without which the much-vaunted globalisation is in danger of itself becoming a life-size catastrophe.

Both a natural and a man-made catastrophe, a *general* catastrophe and not one *specific* to any particular technology or region of the world, which would far exceed the disasters currently covered by the insurance companies—a catastrophe of which the long-term drama of Chernobyl remains emblematic.

So as to avoid in the near future experiencing an integral accident on a planetary scale, an accident capable of incorporating a whole host of incidents and disasters in a chain reaction, we should right now build, inhabit and plan a laboratory of cataclysms —*the technical progress accident museum*—so as to avoid the accident of *substances*, revealed by Aristotle, being succeeded by the *knowledge* accident—that major philosophical catastrophe which genetic engineering, coming on the heels of atomic power, bears within it.

Whether we like it or not, globalisation is today the fateful mark of a finitude. Paraphrasing Paul Valéry, we might assert without fear of contradiction that "the time of the finite world is coming to an end" and that there is an urgent need to assert that knowledge marks the finitude of man, just as ecology marks that of his geophysical environment.

At the very moment when some are requesting, in an open letter to the President of the French Republic, that he create a "Museum of the Twentieth Century" in Paris[2], it seems appropriate to enquire not only into the historical sequence of the events of that fateful century, but also into the fundamentally catastrophic nature of those events.

If, indeed, "time is the accident of accidents,"[3] the museums of history are already an anticipation of the time of that *integral accident* which the twentieth century foreshadowed, on the pretext of scientific revolution or ideological liberation.

All museology requires a museography, and the question of the presentation of *the harm done by Progress* has not received any kind of answer; it therefore falls to us, as a primordial element of the project, to provide one. At this point we have to acknowledge that it is not so much in history books or in the press that this particular historical laboratory has been prefigured, as in radio, cinema newsreel and, above all, television.

Since cinema is *time exhibiting itself*, as the sequences succeed each other, so with television, it is the pace of its "trans-border" ubiquity that disrupts the history in the making before our eyes.

General history has, as a result, experienced a new type of accident, the accident of its perception **at first hand** (de visu): a "cinematic"—and soon to be "digital"—perception which modifies its meaning, its customary rhythm—the rhythm of almanacs and calendars or, in other words, that of *the long run*—in favour of the *ultra-short* timescale of that televisual instantaneity which is revolutionizing our view of the world.

"With speed man has invented new types of accident… The fate of the motorist has become pure chance," wrote Gaston Rageot in the nineteen-thirties[4].

What are we to say, today, of *the major accident of audiovisual speed* and hence of the fate of the innumerable hosts of TV viewers?

Other than that, with that speed, it is history which is becoming "accidental"—through the sudden pile-up of facts, through events which were once successive, but are now simultaneous, cannoning into one another, in spite of the distances and time intervals that used to be required for their interpretation.

Let us imagine, for example, the probable damage that will be done to the authenticity of the testimony of historical actors by the practice of live digital **morphing**.

Speaking of the preponderant influence of film on the conception of contemporary art, Dominique Païni has stated: "For a long time, the cinema came out of the other arts, now it is the plastic arts which come out of it."

But in fact it is *the whole of history that comes out of cinematic acceleration*, out of this movement in cinema and television!

Hence the ravages wrought by the circulation of images, this constant concertinaing, this constant pile-up of dramatic scenes from everyday life on the evening news. And even if the written press has always been more interested in derailed trains than the ones that run on time, it is with the coming of the audiovisual media that we have been able to look on, thunderstruck, at the **overexposure of accidents**, of catastrophes of all kinds—not to mention wars.

Where the broadcasting of horror is concerned, television has, since the end of the last century, been the (live) site of a constant raising of the stakes and, particularly with the increase in **live coverage**, it has provided us with an instantaneous transmission of cataclysms and incidents that have broadly anticipated disaster movies.

Moreover, after the standardization of opinion, which began in the nineteenth century, we are now seeing the sudden *synchronization* of emotions.

TV channels' competition for viewers has turned the catastrophic accident into a scoop, if not indeed a fantastic spectacle which all pursue with equal vigour.

When Guy Debord spoke of the "society of the spectacle," he omitted to mention that this scenarization of life was organized around sexuality and violence; a sexuality which the sixties claimed to liberate, whereas what was actually happening was a progressive abolition of societal inhibitions, regarded by the Situationists as so many unbearable straitjackets.

As was so well expressed at the time by one of the officials of the Festival du film fantastique d'Avoriaz, "*At last death will have replaced sex and the serial killer the Latin lover!*"

Television—a "museum of horrors" or a "tunnel of death"—has, then, gradually transformed itself into a kind of *altar of human sacrifice,* using and abusing the terrorist scene and serial massacres; it now plays more on repulsion than on seduction.

From the death twenty years ago—allegedly "live on air"—of a little Columbian girl being swallowed by mud, to the execution this winter of little Mohammed struck down beside his father, when it comes to making horror banal, any pretext will serve.

By contrast, as we may recall, the mass media in the old Soviet Union never reported accidents or violent incidents. With the exception of natural catastrophes, which it would have been difficult to pass over, the media systematically censored any *deviations from the norm*, allowing only visions of a radiant future to filter through… until Chernobyl.

However, when it comes to censorship, liberalism and totalitarianism each had their particular method for stifling the true facts. For the former, the aim was, even then, to overexpose the viewer to the incessant repetition of tragedies; the latter, by contrast, opted for underexposure and the radical occultation of any singularity.

Two panic reactions, but an identical outcome: *censorship by illumination*—a fateful blinding by the light—for the democratic West, and *censorship by the prohibition of any divergent representation*—the darkness and fog of wilful blindness—for the dogmatic East.

So, just as there is a Richter scale of seismic catastrophes, so there is, surreptitiously, a scale of media catastrophes, the clearest effect of which is to cause, on the one hand, resentment against the perpetrators and, on the other, an effect of exemplarity, which leads, where terrorism is concerned, to the reproduction of the disaster, thanks to its dramaturgical amplification. So much is this the case that to Nietzsche's study of the *birth of tragedy* we need to add the analysis of this media tragedy, in which the perfect synchronization of the collective emotion of TV viewers might be said to play the role of the ancient chorus—though no longer on the scale of the theatre at Epidauros, but on the life-size scale of entire continents.

It is clearly here that the museum of the accident has its place…

The *media scale* of catastrophes and cataclysms that dress the world in mourning is, in fact, so vast that it must necessarily make the amplitude of the perceptual field the first stage of a new understanding—no longer solely that of the *ecology of risks* in the face of environmental pollution, but that of an *ethology of threats* in terms of the mystification of opinion, of a pollution of public emotion.

A pollution that always paves the way for intolerance followed by vengeance. In other words for a barbarism and chaos which quickly overwhelm human societies, as has recently been demonstrated by the massacres and genocides, those fruits of the baneful propaganda of the "media of hatred."

After a period of waiting for the "*integral accident*" to occur, we are seeing the forceps birth of a "catastrophism" that bears no relation whatever (we really must make no mistake about this) to that of the "millenarian" obscurantism of yesteryear, but which requires just as much in the way of precautions, in the way of that Pascalian "subtlety" which our organs of mass information so cruelly lack!

Since one catastrophe may conceal another, *if the major accident is indeed the consequence of the speed of acceleration of the phenomena* engendered by progress, it is certainly time, in these early years of the twenty-first century, to take what is happening, what is emerging unexpectedly before our eyes and analyse it wisely. Hence the imperative need now to exhibit the accident.

In conclusion, one final example: just recently, astronomers have begun to list and observe the asteroids and meteorites which are heading towards Earth.

These so-called NEAs, **near-earth asteroids** some ten metres in diameter, clearly represent a threat of collision with our planet.

The last impact was the one which took place in 1908 in Siberia, above the Tunguska, which exploded at 8,000 metres and ravaged an area of almost 2,000 square kilometres.

In order to attempt to prevent such a cosmic catastrophe recurring, this time over inhabited areas, a working group has been formed.

With support from the *International Astronomical Union*, this team has invented a scale of risk named the Torino Scale, after the city of Turin where this course of action was adopted in 1999. Ranking dangers on a scale from zero to ten, it takes into account the mass, velocity and presumed trajectory of the heavenly body in question.

Five zones are identified by the scientists: the *White Zone*, where there is no chance (*sic*) of the object reaching Earth; the *Green Zone*, where there would be a tiny probability of contact; the *Yellow Zone*, where impact is, in fact, probable; the *Orange Zone*, where that probability is great and, finally, the *Red Zone*, where catastrophe is certain[5].

This very first attempt to **exhibit the future accident**—an in no way alarmist illustration of cosmic facts of which our moon bears the marks, not to mention the more than one-kilometre-wide Meteor Crater in Arizona which is frequently visited by American tourists—demonstrates the urgent need to follow up the famous "cabinets of curiosities" of the Renaissance[6] with a twenty-first-century museum of the accident of the future.

Notes

1. *Le Monde*, February 24, 2001.

2. Jacques Julliard, "Chronique" (*Le Nouvel Observateur*, January 30, 2002).

3. Aristotle, *Physics*.

4. Gaston Rageot, *L'homme standard* (Paris: Plon, 1928), a work contemporaneous with Paul Morand's *L'homme pressé* (Paris: Gallimard, 1941)

5. Pierre Barthélémy, "Les asteroïdes constituent le principal risque naturel pour la Terre" (*Le Monde*, June 28, 2002).

6. Patrick Mauriès, *Les Cabinets de curiosités* (Paris: Gallimard, 2002).

Text translated from French by Chris Turner

March 1, 1896, Paris, France
Image showing two marks left on a photographic plate
by the radiation of uranium salt:
discovery of radioactivity by Henri Becquerel
© Cosmos/Science Photo Library

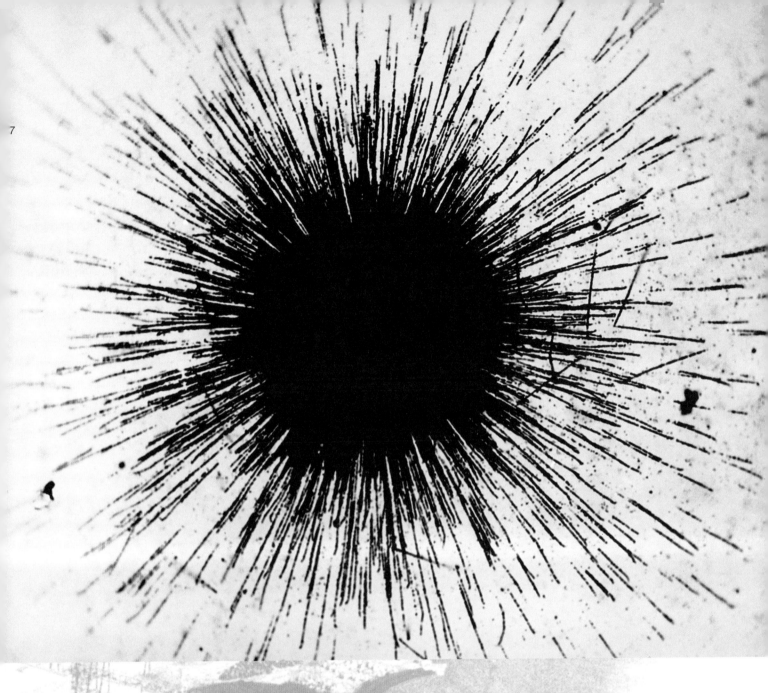

December 26, 1898, Paris, France
Image showing the mark left by the radioactivity of radium alpha particles
on a photographic plate: discovery of radium by Marie Curie.
This radiation is one million times more intense than that of uranium
© Cosmos/Science Photo Library

Preamble to catastrophe

March 28, 1979, Three Mile Island, Pennsylvania, United States
Nuclear accident followed by radioactive leaks around the plant:
evacuation of the site
© AFP/UPI

"Reality outstrips consciousness: the word 'catastrophe'
applied to the event of Chernobyl is insufficient, it obscures
the sense of the tragedy. No adequate term has yet
been invented.Chernobyl is a an accident of knowledge, both
post-conceptual and post-scientific. It is necessary
to find other supports in this world than those of science."

Svetlana Aleksievich

January 1996, Chernobyl, Ukraine
View of the interior
of the protective sarcophagus built
after the 1986 catastrophe
© Epix/Corbis Sygma

October 1, 1986, Chernobyl, Ukraine
Repairs being carried out on the
Chernobyl nuclear plant in the Ukraine,
following a major explosion on
April 26, 1986: it affected more than
3.2 million people—according to official
statistics—and sent radioactive
clouds all over Europe
© AFP/TASS/Zufarov

June 26, 2000, London, United Kingdom
First working model of the human DNA structure
© AFP/EPA/PA/Matthew Fearn

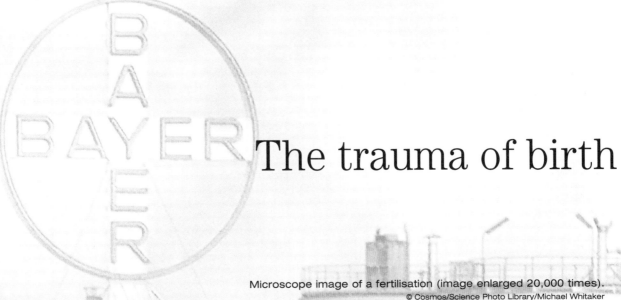

The trauma of birth

Microscope image of a fertilisation (image enlarged 20,000 times).
© Cosmos/Science Photo Library/Michael Whitaker

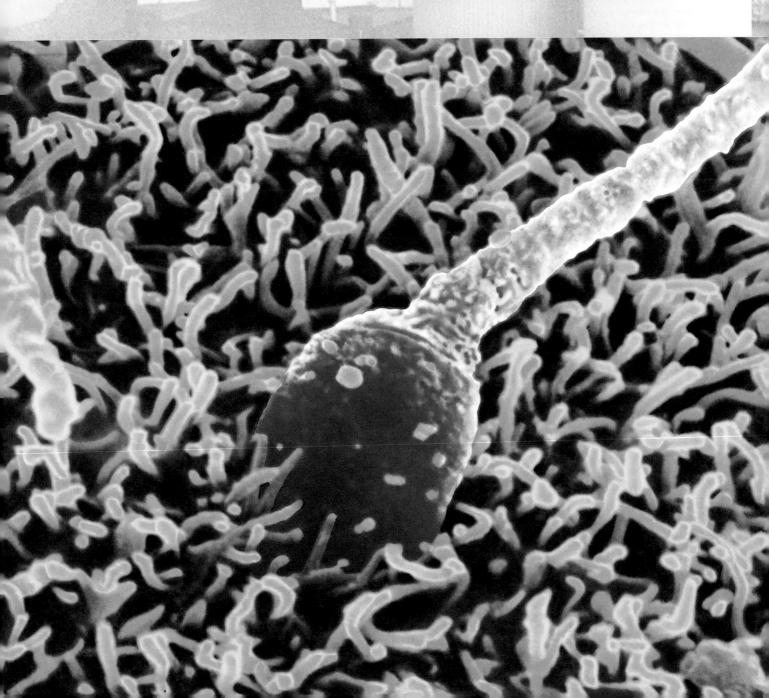

January 5, 1966, Feyzin, Rhône, France
Explosion at the Feyzin refinery; a piece of metal was thrown
several dozen metres by the explosion of one of the spherical reservoirs:
17 people killed and 84 injured
© AFP

July 28, 1976, Seveso, Sicily, Italy
Cultivation of corn in a zone polluted by a dioxin gas
leak from the Icmesa factory near Seveso
© AFP

COMUNI MEDA E SEVESO

ZONA
INFESTATA
da
sostanze tossiche

DIVIETO

TOCCARE O INGERIRE PRODOTTI
ORTOFRUTTICOLI, EVITANDO
CONTATTI CON VEGETAZIONE,
TERRA E ERBE IN GENERE.

L'UFFICIALE SANITARIO   I SINDACI

November 21, 2001, Krefeld, Germany
Fire on a cargo vessel at the Bayer chemical company's wharf:
toxic fumes in the area and nitric acid leaking into the Rhine
© AFP/Roland Weihrauch

December 4, 1984, Bhopal, India
Poison gas leak from the Union Carbide factory:
2,500 people killed and more than 10,000 injured
© AFP/Bedi

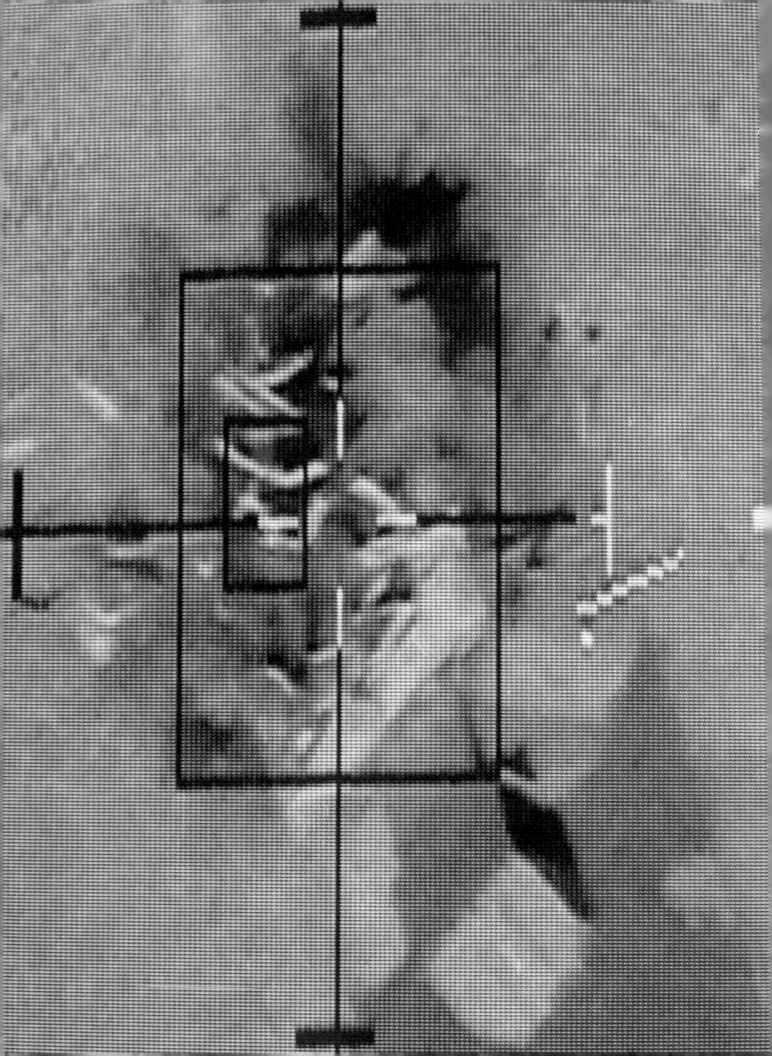

War crime or ecological crime?

February 9, 1991, Irak
Burning of an oil storage zone during the Gulf war in 1991:
16 tanks measuring 90 metres in diameter and 500,000 cubic metres of oil on fire
© Cosmos/Science Photo Library/Spot Image/Nigel Press Associates

January 19, 1991, Bagdad, Irak
Sights of a French jet-fighter targeting
an Iraqi ammunition depot during the Gulf war
© AFP / SIRPA

1991, Kuwait
Oil spilled in the desert by the retreating Iraki army
© Magnum/Steve McCurry

March 14, 1991, Kuwait
Burning oil wells damaged by retreating Iraki soldiers
in southern Kuwait: 727 wells torched
and 8 billion barrels of oil poured into the sea,
vast contamination of the atmosphere
© AFP/Nicolas Kamm

Above:
April 1, 1989, Valdez, Alaska, United States
Oil skimming operation after the wreck of the tanker
Exxon Valdez, which ran aground on March 24,
spilling 11 million gallons of crude oil into the North Pacific
© AFP/Chris Wilkins

March 17, 1978, Portsall, Finistère, France
Wreck of the tanker Amoco Cadiz: thousands of tons of oil
spilled into the ocean around Brittany
© AFP/Jean-Pierre Prevel

December 13, 1999, Brest, France
Sinking of the Maltase tanker Erica:
contamination of the coast
of Brittany a few days after
© AFP/Marine Nationale

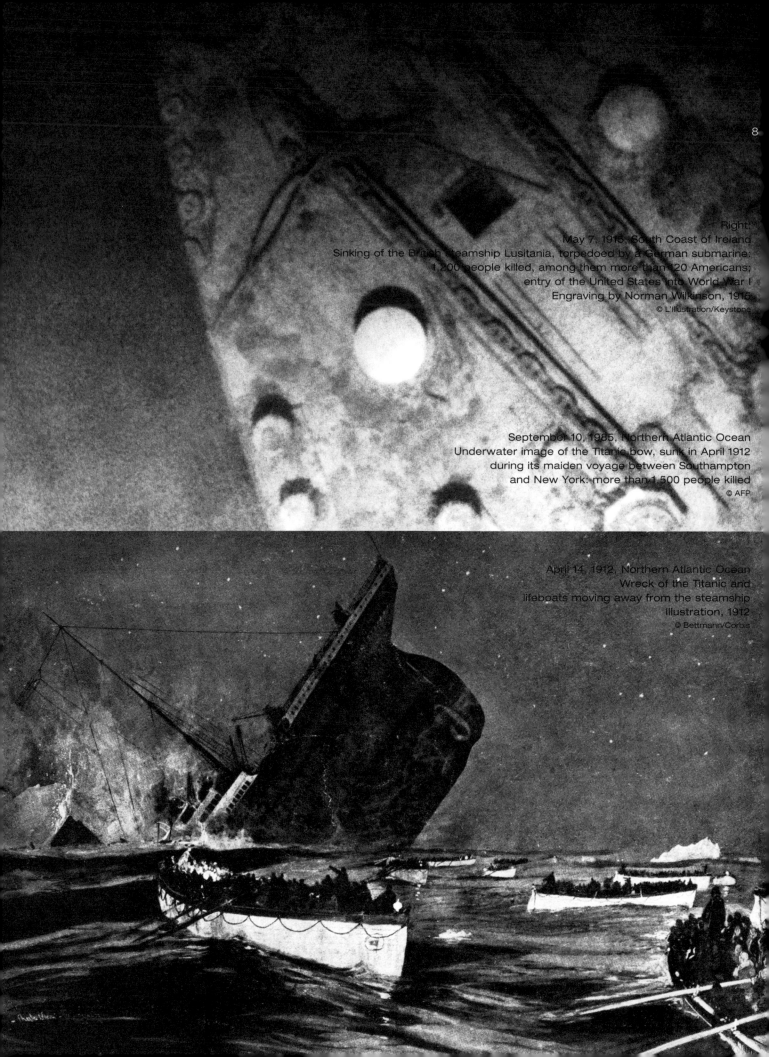

Right:
May 7, 1915, South Coast of Ireland
Sinking of the British steamship Lusitania, torpedoed by a German submarine;
1,200 people killed, among them more than 120 Americans;
entry of the United States into World War I
Engraving by Norman Wilkinson, 1915
© L'Illustration/Keystone

September 10, 1985, Northern Atlantic Ocean
Underwater image of the Titanic bow, sunk in April 1912
during its maiden voyage between Southampton
and New York: more than 1,500 people killed
© AFP

April 14, 1912, Northern Atlantic Ocean
Wreck of the Titanic and
lifeboats moving away from the steamship
Illustration, 1912
© Bettmann/Corbis

81

March 7, 1987, Zeebrugge, Belgium
Wreck of the ferry Harald of Free Enterprise caused by a leak
in the vehicle deck. 200 passengers feared dead
© AFP/Boris Horvat

Oceans nullified

8

Aralsk, Kazakhstan
Overexploitation of waters: ships resting on sand
after the retreat of the Aral Sea
© AFP/Victor Vasenin

July 30, 1999, Santiago, Chile
Pollution hovers over Santiago, capital of Chile:
5.5 million people endure atmospheric pollution
© AFP/Macarena Minguell

Right:
March 6, 2000, Rio de Janeiro, Brazil
Oxygen depletion caused by heat and water pollution:
in two days, some 100 tons of fish have died
in the Rodrigo de Freitas Lake
© AFP/Antonio Scorza

3

Unity of place:
8 years after the Boeing bombing, the
sanitary catastrophe

March 3, 2001, Lockerbie, Scotland
Some 300 cattle and 400 sheep infected
with foot and mouth disease are incinerated in Lockerbie
© AFP/Odd Andersen

The future of the accident

"The world of the future will be an ever more demanding struggle
against the limitations of our intelligence."

Norbert Wiener[1]

Paul Virilio

No gain without a corresponding loss. If to invent the substance is, indirectly, to invent the accident, then the more powerful and efficient the invention, the more dramatic the accident.

Eventually the fateful day will come when the progress of knowledge becomes intolerable, not just because of its misuse but also because of its effects—the very power of its negativity.

This was confirmed to us throughout the twentieth century, first by the nuclear, then by the thermonuclear arms race, in which the arms themselves ultimately became unusable and condemned the protagonists to deterrence—an all-out deterrence.

The very power of atomic weaponry also marks the ultimate limit of that power, which has suddenly become impotence… Here it is the fearsome uselessness of this type of weaponry that constitutes the accident.

Rather than really fight, military staffs engage in imaginary exercises of a zero-sum "war-game," in which virtuality is merely the mark of the political inconsequentiality of nations, since the consequences are no longer really of any importance, being both too enormous to be apprehended seriously and too fearsome to be properly tested… except by a madman—by the prospective perpetrator of a *suicide attack on humanity*.

In this connection, let us attend to what Friedrich Nietzsche has to say in his essay, *The Birth of Tragedy*, written in the years following the Franco-Prussian War of 1870: "… a culture based on the principles of science must be destroyed when it begins to grow *illogical,* that is, to retreat before its own consequences. Our art reveals this universal distress."[2]

If, indeed, "in tragedy the state of civilization is suspended,"[3] then with it the entire span of beneficial knowledge is swept away. Therefore, in total war, the sudden militarization of science, required for the presumed victory of the opponents, reverses all logic and political wisdom, to the point where the ancient philo-sophy is succeeded by the absurdity of a phil-anoia[4] that is liable to destroy the knowledge accumulated over the centuries… "Human power, excessively increased, transforms itself then into a cause of ruin,"[5] tipping over the whole of the culture of nations into the void of lost causes—causes irremediably lost, in the case of defeat or of victory, since it is not possible to uninvent a knowledge both terroristic and sacrilegious to the scientific intelligence.

So, just as there are spells of bad weather in nature, there are also periods of bad weather in culture and we would need a positive "meteorology" of invention to attempt to avoid *the storms of the artifice of the Progress of knowledge*—that spirit which generates the extreme potentiation of our instruments and our substances, and, conjointly, of industrial or postindustrial accidents; I am thinking in the first instance, of genetics and information technology, following upon the depredations wrought by atomic progress, the atrocious truth of which was revealed to us first by Hiroshima, then by Chernobyl.

"It is astonishing what those who can do everything cannot do," declared Mme Swetchine in the nineteenth century[6]. This aphorism sums up perfectly the paradox of the twentieth century and its *serial revolutions*, like so many weapons deployed against the intelligibility of the world.

Today, at this very beginning of the twenty-first century, when the globalisation we hear so widely praised is, first and foremost, the forbidden fruit of the tree of knowledge (in other words, of the so-called "information revolution") the predator is giving way to the exterminator, and simple capitalism to terrorism.

Since extermination is indeed the illogical conclusion of accumulation, the *suicidal State* is no longer simply *psychological*, linked to the mentality of a number of disturbed individuals, but *sociological* and political, to the extent that the generalized accident announced by Nietzsche now incorporates that panic dimension in which the *philosophy of the Enlightenment* gives way to the love of the *folie des grandeurs,* a philanoia of gigantic proportions. This is indeed what this knowledge accident is, which complements the accident of substance that comes out of techno-scientific research.

And if there are three dimensions to matter—mass, energy and information, then after the long series of material and energy-related accidents of the last century, the time is now at hand of the *logical accident*—and even the biological accident, as we see the *teratological research* of genetic engineering.

"The machines have declared war on God," wrote Karl Kraus famously, as the butchery of World War One was beginning[7]... But how do things stand today, in the age of a globalisation so vaunted by the advocates of Progress?

The globalisation of knowledge, a product of the telecommunications revolution, has not only reduced the field of human activity to nothing thanks to the synchronization of inter-activity, but is causing a historical mutation in the very notion of the accident.

The *local*, precisely situated accident has suddenly given way to the possibility of a *global* accident, which would no longer merely concern "substances"—the substance of the world in the age of the real time of exchanges—but the knowledge we have of reality, that view of the world which previously underlay our sciences.

So, after the accident of substance, with the century that is now upon us, we are inaugurating an unparalleled accident, an accident of reality, the accident of space and time, and of substantial matter totally unknown to the cynics, but which the relativity physicists gradually brought in with them in the course of total war.

"*Time is merely an illusion*" declared Einstein, during that period separating the First World War from the Second. An accident of historical knowledge, or in other words, of the perception of things—a positive de-realization, this, the product of a reality now in accelerated flight, like the galaxies in the expansion of the universe, a de-realization the ravages of which were already sensed by Werner Heisenberg when he wrote fifty years ago: "No one knows what will be real for men at the end of the wars that are now beginning."[8]

Finally, after the implosion of the Cold War between East and West, globalisation is, first and foremost, a kind of *journey to the centre of the earth*, in the darkening gloom of a temporal compression which closes off the human race's living space once and for all, a thing some utopians have termed the *sixth continent*, though it is simply the hypercentre of our environment.

Both origin and end of a world that is now foreclosed, where everyone is unceasingly attracted by this *central region* without spatial or temporal extension, which is simply the culmination, the terminal of that *acceleration of reality* which crushes our five continents and seven seas into each other, but, most importantly, crushes together the nations and peoples of the whole world.

A telluric compression of the history of humanity, the scope of which registers on no seismograph, in spite of the ecologists; the compression of that cataclysm in which everything is telescoped, crashes into everything else at every moment, in which all distances are reduced to nothing, smashed by the accident of the real time of interactivity;

a quaking of the whole Earth, where events are no longer anything but *simultaneous, untimely accidents* on the surface of an excessively compressed celestial object, and where gravity and atmospheric pressure are further reinforced by the instantaneous synchronization of exchanges.

At this level of disquiet, ecology is not so much that of nature as the ecology of culture and its maturing ethological catastrophes. Indeed, with the swallowing-up of proportions, periods and scales of time, the instantaneous abolition of all intervals in favour of immediacy, the *pollution of the distances* of the globe's life-size scale teaches us infinitely more than the *pollution of the substances* of nature about the drama, the tragedy of future knowledge. In the fearful compression of the extremities of a once-gigantic world towards the Centre, the *hypercentre of the only habitable planet in the solar system,* "Nature can rely on Progress; it will avenge it for the outrage it has perpetrated on it."[9]

In conclusion, let us ask three questions: *must science reassure? Must science,* a contrario, *frighten?* And, lastly, *is science inhuman?*[10] These questions all cast considerable light on the famous "crisis of Progress", as they do also on the, in no way subsidiary, crisis of the recent mediatization of discoveries—that "scientific expressionism" to which certain madmen/scientists subscribe, such as the gynaecologist Severino Antinori, the "Doctor Strangelove" of assisted procreation, or the academic cancer specialist Friedhelm Hermann, accused in Autumn 1999 by a German commission responsible for detecting fraud in science labs of having falsified his team's results, occasioning, as the specialised press put it, a veritable "scientific Chernobyl!"[11]

Let us recall here that scientific research cannot avail itself of the freedom of expression of the sensational press without ending, sooner or later, in the philanoia of a science not just bereft of conscience, but *bereft of sense*!

Yesterday the atomic bomb, today the information bomb, tomorrow the genetic bomb? When, in August 2001, professor Antinori presented to the American Academy of Sciences his plan to see some two hundred babies born by reproductive cloning, promising the "parents" *perfect children*, even if that meant eliminating the *imperfect* ones, what is this but demiurgical raving? Proof, if any were needed, that in science, as elsewhere, *the worst sometimes does happen*[12].

With the radioactive fall-out of Chernobyl, genetically modified organisms, the cloning of human beings etc—the scientific experts now stand at the heart of the controversies of these early years of the third millennium. Hence the recent creation of *agencies specializing in risk management*, in order to attempt to predict the improbable and the unthinkable in scientific and technical matters, since we have for several decades now been *defenceless* in the face of major risks affecting the biological and social equilibrium of humanity[13]. From this particular standpoint of the "knowledge accident", it is not so much the number of victims that stands out as the very nature of the risk being run. By contrast with road, rail or air accidents, the risk is no longer quantifiable and statistically *predictable*—it has become inexpressible and deeply *unpredictable*, to the point of causing unparalleled risk to emerge, risk no longer located simply in the ecological but in the eschatological dimension, since it affects the mind's power of anticipation, i.e. rationality itself[14].

"*The ruin of the soul*," wrote Rabelais, speaking of knowledge without conscience—and this gives us another perspective today for approaching the problems of the end of life at a period when the question of the euthanasia of humanity is on the agenda, as an inevitable consequence of a *twilight of the grounds* which seems to occasion no disquiet.

Notes

1. Norbert Wiener, *God and Golem Inc.* (London/Cambridge, Mass: MIT Press, 1964), p. 69.
2. Nietzsche, *The Birth of Tragedy and other writings* (Cambridge: Cambridge University Press, 1999).
3. *Ibid.*
4. A love of madness.
5. Henri Atlan, *La Science est-elle inhumaine?* (Paris: Éditions Bayard Centurion, collection 'Temps d'une Question', 2002).
6. Victor Hugo, *Things Seen.* Madame Swetchine, a friend of Brother Henri Lacordaire, was a Christian-Democrat.
7. *In these great times* (Manchester: Carcanet, 1984), p. 80.
8. Werner Heisenberg, *Physics and Philosophy.*
9. Kraus, *op. cit.*, p. 56.
10. Henri Atlan, *op.cit.*
11. "Hermann, docteur es fraude" (*Libération*, October 26, 1999).
12. "Le savant fou" (*La Croix*, August 8, 2002).
13. Hatchuel, Armand *et al., Experts in Organizations* (Berlin: Walter de Gruyter, 1995).
14. After the atomic strategy known as "du faible au fort" (from the weak to the strong), which justified the extension of the concept of deterrence between states with the French *force de frappe*, 1990 saw a campaign begun for the strategy known as "du faible au fou" (from the weak to the mad), as a means of tackling the problems of nuclear proliferation. See Ben Cramer, *Le nucléaire dans tous ses états* (Paris: Éditions Alias, 2002).

Text translated from French by Chris Turner

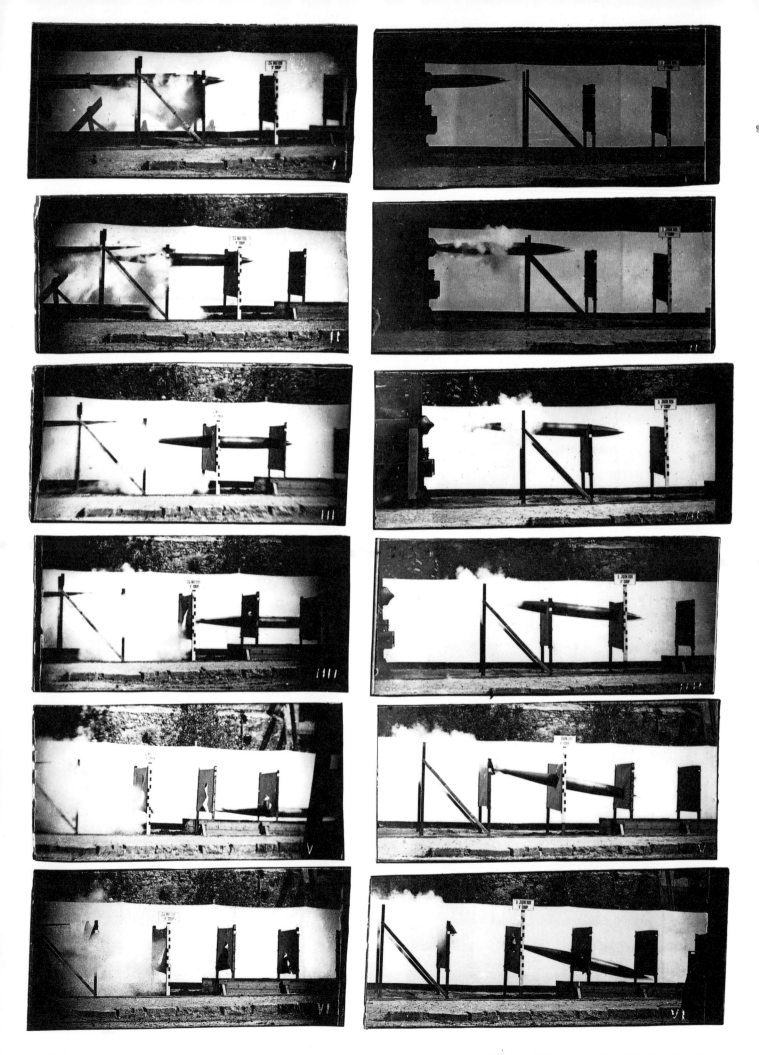

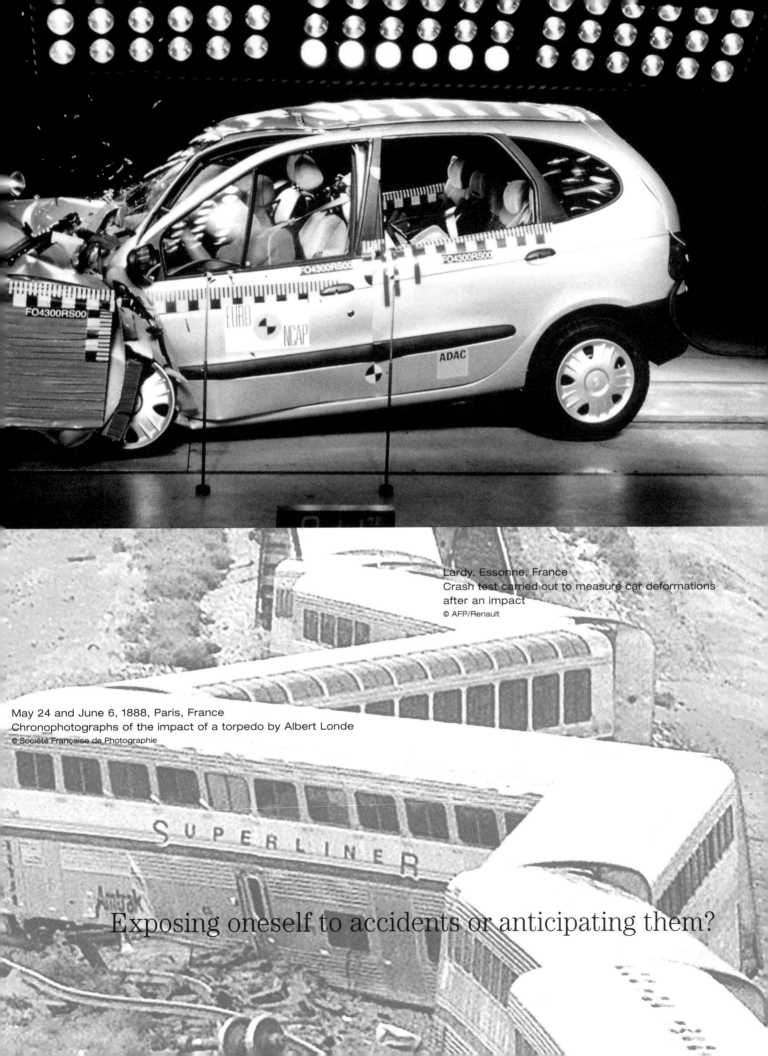

Lardy, Essonne, France
Crash test carried out to measure car deformations
after an impact
© AFP/Renault

May 24 and June 6, 1888, Paris, France
Chronophotographs of the impact of a torpedo by Albert Londe
© Société Française de Photographie

SUPERLINER

Exposing oneself to accidents or anticipating them?

March 24, 1999, Nairobi, Kenya
Derailment of railway carriages: 32 people
killed and at least 100 others injured
© AFP/Alexander Joe

August 9, 1997, Kingman, Arizona, United States
Derailment of a passenger train after passing
over a railroad bridge that was apparently damaged
by a storm: more than 100 people injured
© AFP/John Gurzinski

From the excess of speed to the speed
of excess: the inevitable accident

June 3, 1998, Eschede, Germany
Train derailment in Eschede after a car,
falling from an overpass, plunged onto the speeding train:
at least 70 people feared killed
© AFP/Ingo Wagner

October 22, 1895, Paris, France
Train accident in the Montparnasse Railway Station
© Roger-Viollet

The deliberate accident: the end of the Zeppelin makes for the rise of airplane travel

May 6, 1937, New Jersey, United States
The giant German airship Hindenburg bursts into flames
over the New Jersey coast: 33 people killed
© AFP

August 28, 1988, Ramstein, Federal Republic of Germany
Jets of the Italian acrobatic squad colliding in mid-air during an air show:
70 people killed and more than 450 injured
© AFP/Martin Füger

June 2, 2001, Pacific Ocean
Loss of control of the NASA X-43A hypersonic research aircraft
after a test flight at the speed of Mach 7:
volontary explosion induced 8 seconds after
© AFP/NASA

July 25, 2000, Roissy, France
Air France Concorde taking off with the tail end
on fire, before crashing into a hotel in Gonesse
a few minutes after: 113 people killed
© AFP

December 7, 1997
Irkoutsk, Siberia, Russian Confederation
Part of the fuselage of a military cargo plane
that crashed into a housing area after
taking off with 100 tons of fuel and two fighter jets
on board: 100 people killed
© AFP/Anatoly Maltsev

The abnormal size of the plane's fuselage
foreshadows the large-scale accident

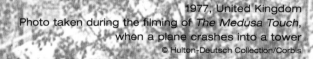

1977, United Kingdom
Photo taken during the filming of *The Medusa Touch*,
when a plane crashes into a tower
© Hulton-Deutsch Collection/Corbis

July 2, 2002, Kloten, Switzerland
Radar controlling in-flight collision risks.
The night before, a pilot did not react
to the repeated warnings of the control tower
and two planes crashed in flight
© AFP/Franco Greco

July 31, 1997,
Newark, New Jersey, United States
Smoke rising from a
Federal Express cargo plane
that crashed upon landing
© AFP/Jon Levy

The writing of disaster

November 19, 1997, New York, United States
Reconstitution of the TWA Boeing 747
that mysteriously crashed after take-off
on July 17, 1996: 230 people killed
© AFP/Jon Levy

The horizon of expectation

"Poetic creation is the creation of expectation."

Paul Valéry

Paul Virilio

The sense of insecurity that has appeared over the last ten years is not just linked to so-called "anti-social acts" affecting urban dwellers, but is, it seems, the symptom of a new horizon of expectation, the third of its kind after the horizons of expectation of "revolution" and "war". I am referring to the expectation of the integral accident, that major accident, which is not merely ecological—the one that has been present in people's minds for the last thirty years or so—but, above all, an eschatological accident—the accident specific to a world henceforth foreclosed, in what is termed "globalisation". There is no end today to the debating of this phenomenon, both hoped-for and feared, as though the *anthropological horizon* of ideas and ideals seemed all at once blocked, both by the foreclosure of a geometric confinement and by the suddenness of the global time of the interactivity of exchanges.

We are in fact waiting for something, in enormous expectation of something, and present horror films are not just the formulaic products of Hollywood cinema and the desire systematically to frighten viewers, as though there were a Hell at the heart of the world. No, what we are seeing here is the recent emergence of the *sense of the End of the world*—in no sense an apocalyptic or millenarian End, synonymous with an End of History, but, more simply, *an End of Geography*, as though the all-too-famous consumer society had ended up consuming planetary space-time, a role in which it has been duly replaced by the recently developed communication-based society.

Whereas ancient societies were almost all agoraphobic, shut in on themselves in their *closed cities* and their excessive rings of fortifications, postmodern societies seem suddenly claustrophobic, as though the *open city* of our age led, in the end, to exclusion…

"*Completion is a limit*", declared Aristotle in his second axiom… The foreclosed world of economic and political globalisation is, in effect, the ultimate limit of the geopolitics of nations, and people's sense of panic insecurity, together with the gigantic population movements of the coming repopulation of the continents, are proof of this. A warning that has cost us nothing, but one our democracies should take into account before future tyrants use it to their advantage.

So, in this twenty-first century, alongside the pollution of substances (of air, water, fauna and flora), there is emerging the sudden pollution of the distances and intervals which make up the very density of our daily reality; of that *real space* of our activities which the interactivity of the *real time* of instant exchanges has just abolished.

And here the "grey ecology" of the pollution of the natural scale rounds out the "green ecology" of the pollution—by chemical or other products—of nature.

We might speak here of the birth of two currents of thought which are not at all antagonistic, but complementary: the substantialists (or, if one prefers, the materialists) and the accidentalists (or, to use another name, the spiritualists).

How could one fail to see, indeed, that *the first political movement concerned with the generalized Accident* is the one usually referred to as "the Green movement"?

A movement which is, admittedly, more concerned with the pollution of material substances than with the pollution of time distances, which is reducing to nothing, or almost nothing, the extent and duration of our habitat, that human environment which, nonetheless, apart from its material nature, also possesses irreducible geophysical dimensions and proportions.

Proportions as vital as water or the air we breathe for those who are already afraid that *the Great Confinement* of the seventeenth century (which was, according to Michel Foucault, at the origin of the Enlightenment revolution) might be reproduced— though this time not on the carceral scale of prisons or asylums, but *on the scale of the whole world.*

Hence this urgent need for a second political movement of the integral Accident which would be complementary to the first, an eschatological party to stand alongside today's officially recognized ecological one.

Like the high and low notes in stereophony, this dual ecopolitical movement would create a field effect, a relief that is henceforth indispensable both to the Right and the Left of our democratic assemblies since, as everyone senses, this classical political representation cannot be lastingly sustained without a genuinely *geopolitical* definition of ecology—in other words, without taking account not just of the famous "imperative of responsibility," which is incumbent upon our elected representatives, but also of the "precautionary principle" and the principle of vigilance on the part of scientific and other officials.

In this sense, the crisis—or, rather, the accident—of "representative democracy" has nothing transient about it, since the *citizen/TV-viewer* cannot be governed like a nineteenth century reader or lecture-goer, his/her vision of the world being quite other. Some ecologists, such as the Grünen in Germany, have recently come to understand this, being concerned now to interpret the very notion of globalisation better—not just as an economic, but as an ecological phenomenon[1].

"The civilized world must take seriously the growing threat of terror on a catastrophic scale," declared George W. Bush on March 15. Seriously, yes, but not in any sense tragically. To do that would be to lapse into *nihilism* and to pass without transition from the euphoria of the consumer society to the neurasthenia of a derelict one, as perceived by Karl Kraus, when he wrote in 1914: *"Thrown into the neurasthenia of hatred, everything is* true."[2]

How can we not realize to what extent the drama has been taken out of the political game today, abased as it is by this "new idea" of a so-called *happiness* conveyed by the shadow cast by the Revolution of the Enlightenment, but also by Terror? How can we not be aware of our incapacity to take on board the major risks, the prospective great break-downs, before which our hedonistic culture is basically disarmed?

Geopolitical ecology would also be this: to confront the unforeseeable, that Medusa of a technical progress which is literally exterminating the whole world.

Some in authority already take the view that the great wrenches the "geopolitical economy" needs to undergo are impossible without a horrendous world crisis which, terrifying everyone, would force the nations and peoples of the world into a sudden global realization of danger. This is to forget, rather quickly, that fear is a poor counsellor, as all dictatorships have proven since antiquity.

Since the last century, everyone has known from experience that dictatorships are not "natural accidents". They are created with the aid of multiple unacknowledged complicities, particularly the complicity of collective emotion. Who can forget the massive fear over *Lebensraum* generated by the naturalistic ideology of the Nazi movement?

We may note here a minor event which is particularly revealing of the widespread general sense of unease: a National Union of Catastrophe Victims has recently been created in France bringing together up to sixty support associations for accident victims, from the floods at Abbeville to the Toulouse explosion, taking in road accidents on the way.

This **National Union** now poses as the sole partner in discussion with the public authorities. Prefiguring a future *eschatological party*, this union of associations offers a glimpse of the possible emergence not just of a co-ordinating body for "trade unions of victims", but, above all, for a party of "life's accident victims" which would replace the party of the *exploited workers* that is currently on the path to extinction—those workers whose socialism not so long ago represented the *demand for justice*.

But here the rampant ideology is less that of a legitimate duty of care to populations and more a "precautionary principle" pushed to the absurd lengths of the myth of *comprehensive insurance*.

"T he idea of protection haunts and fills life," claimed one of the twentieth century's great exterminators. But this paradoxical observation of Adolf Hitler's forces us to review the origin of the various "horizons of expectation" which preceded that of the *Great Accident* of which ecology provides a symptom today.

In fact, since the eighteenth and nineteenth centuries, three types of expectation have succeeded and overlapped with each other without anyone seemingly being affronted by the constant *shift to extremes* they have represented.

In the eighteenth century it was, first, revolution or, more exactly, the American and French revolutions that were to lead to the succession of political upheavals with which we are familiar, right down to the implosion of the Soviet Union at the end of the twentieth century, not forgetting the nihilistic revolution of Nazism.

Sustained by techno-scientific progress, these political revolutions brought about the host of *energy and industrial* revolutions—revolutions in transport and telecommunications—which need no enumeration here.

As Lenin expertly explained, "The revolution is communism plus electrification."

In parallel with this first "horizon of expectation," the nineteenth century was to contribute to generating the second one—that of war. Beginning with the concept of *Great War*, of which the first global conflict of 1914—after the Napoleonic epic—was to indicate the geopolitical absurdity, then moving on to that other conflict, the Second World War, a *Total War*, in which the enemy would be both the human race as such at Auschwitz and its environment at Hiroshima… not to speak of those forty or so years of the *balance of terror* between East and West, a Third World War between the two antagonistic blocs which remained undeclared on the pretext of "nuclear deterrence", though the *militarization of science* and the arms race in weapons of mass destruction were soon to reveal its atrocious nature.

There is no point, I believe, specifying precisely the close correlation between these horizons of expectation—"war" and "revolution" reinforcing each other mutually, in the name of a technical and political Progress uncontested by all but a few heretical thinkers…

In this connection, let us attend to one of them. "In the nineteenth century, the notion of **revolution as rebellion** rapidly ceased to represent the idea of violent reform in order to remedy a bad state of affairs, and became, rather, the expression of an overturning of that which exists as such, **whatever it may be**. The past becoming the enemy and change in itself becoming the important thing," [3] as Paul Valéry noted in the nineteen-thirties, before completing this statement of fact with the remark, "We are the most routine of peoples, we French, who have made a **routine** of **revolution** itself." [4]

Which is probably one of the unheeded causes of the French defeat of 1940, at a time when the *war of extermination* had long since supplanted the *Enlightenment Revolution* with the *darkness and fog* of totalitarianism.

Yet, during this fateful period for humanity, a small number of women had already glimpsed the truth of what was going on more lucidly than many statesmen. After Simone Weil or Hannah Arendt, let us listen to Brigitte Friang speaking to us of the inter-war years: "Throughout the whole of my childhood I heard talk of war… Films, such as *Verdun, vision d'histoire* [5], whose canon fire haunted my childhood nightmares. Henri de Bournazel and Major Raynal were as familiar to me as Bibi Fricotin or Zig and Puce! [6] This kind of intimate contact is rarely without effect. *War, war! It was the key word, the last word, the leitmotif. It was so much 'bound to happen' that it did.*" [7]

The final say on the matter, we might think. But no. Another word—a witty remark by Pierre Mendès France dating from 1968: "*We are in 1788, but without the revolution to come next year.*" And this was indeed the case. The events of that spring remained "events"—a kind of literary commune and no more… The concept of "revolution" had exhausted its ideological potential and was now nothing more than a muffled disquiet, *the waiting for a nameless catastrophe* in which nascent ecology was soon to take over from waiting for the revolutionary "Great Day," an expectation which was to end in the implosion of the USSR shortly after Chernobyl—a cataclysm premonitory not so much of a radiant future as of a radioactive one.

So ended the twentieth century, after more than two hundred mass wars and hundreds of millions of victims: the First World War producing 15 million dead, the Spanish Civil War 500,000, the Second World War 50 million, the Korean War 4 million, the Iran-Iraq conflict 500,000. As for the Gulf War, the talk is of 200,000 victims and it seems it is not even over yet.

But let us leave *revolution* and *war* and look towards *what is happening now*, what is currently on the way, in order to leave discernment its chance. Beyond ethics, bio-ethics is currently troubled today by the major risks the "revolutionary" bio-technological discoveries pose for the human race, leading tomorrow to the threat of a kind of cellular Hiroshima in which the *genetic bomb* would this time ravage the very form of humankind, the way the atomic bomb in its time devastated the horizon of its environment.

There is no shortage of threats to life here: what with medically assisted procreation, cloning or, alternatively, the right to assisted death and euthanasia, not to speak of biological weapons, everything is in place for the *Great Accident* of the Book of Life.

Since the beginning of 2002, for example, as if symbolically to mark the dawn of the third millennium, Dr. Severino Antinori, whose gynaecological clinic is in Rome, the Eternal City, has just announced, like some latter-day Archangel Gabriel, the coming birth of the first *human clone*—with certain anonymous and carefully concealed reproductive subjects readying themselves, it seems, to give birth by means of the so-called "reproductive cloning" procedure.

So hopes of resurrection and the eternal life of the soul are to be blotted out by the shadows of the paraphernalia of a malign *Genetic Engineering*... The *duplication of the living* is being substituted for the resurrection of the dead, and, suddenly, the good "Dr. Miracle" proclaims that it is between December 2002 and January 2003 that the clone child, the human race's first replicant, will be born... So, why not at Christmas?

By way of conclusion, let us return now to this "sense of insecurity which today afflicts the spirit of the masses" and is already to a great extent conditioning the political life of Western nations.

In spite of the threat of *structural,* and terminal, unemployment for certain categories of population, hit hard by the emergence of automated, postindustrial production, the easily perceptible anxiety seems linked not to this type of exclusion from employment, nor indeed to "anti-social behaviour" and domestic violence, but, much more deeply, to the anxiety of the *failure*—itself *terminal*—of the Progress of knowledge which had until then so characterized the era of industrialization.

In fact, the very first expectation of "revolution" went hand in glove with that of a—both philosophical and scientific—progress that was itself going to be swept away by the whirlwind of war; of a total war, the devastating scale of which was already indicated by the militarization of the economy of nations during the twentieth century, leaving behind it in minds only that sense of fear—and often of hate—that currently characterizes affluent societies. We may, in this connection, attend once again to Karl Kraus: "The subjugation of mankind to the economy has left it only the freedom of hostility."[8]

In 1914, the date of this premonitory statement, we were seeing merely the fateful outline of a new "war economy", a form of economy that was going to ruin only the European nations, whereas in our day, at the beginning of the twenty-first century, we are looking at the concluding phase of this *political economy of disaster*.

Henceforth, as everyone glimpses, fears and dreads, the world is closed—foreclosed—and ecology has suddenly become the third dimension of politics, its very relief. After the city-state and the nation-state, the *oversized federation* of the European or other communities is merely the derisory mask of a geopolitical bankruptcy that goes by the assumed name of globalisation—the "integral accident" of a political economy that has just reached the geophysical limit of its field of action.

Notes

1. "Programme sans couleur pour les Verts" (*Libération*, May 8, 2002).

2. Karl Kraus, *In these Great Times*, p. 78.

3. Paul Valéry, *Cahiers*, II (Paris: Gallimard, 1974).

4. Paul Valéry, *ibid*.

5. A famous documentary by Léon Poirier.

6. These were cartoon-strip characters drawn by Louis Forton and Alain de Saint-Ogan respectively.

7. Brigitte Friang, *Regarde-toi qui meurs* (Paris: Éditions de Félin, 1997).

8. Karl Kraus, *In these Great Times*, p. 75.

Text translated from French by Chris Turner

December 22, 1988, Lockerbie, Scotland
Debris of the Pan Am Boeing 747 cockpit, the day after its in-flight explosion
caused by a bomb: 270 people killed
© AFP/Letkey

PI/1353

PI/911

PI/1232

PI/1806

PK/2075

PK/1310A

PI/1808   PI/1807   PI/1803

PI/1388   PI/1420   PI/1431   PI/1466   PI/1487   PI/1488   PI/1538

PI/1545   PI/1548   PI/1552   PI/1564   PI/1565   PI/1589   PI/1590   PI/1591

PT/22

PI/1643   PI/1644   PT/24   PT/25   PT/68

Autopsy of an accident

Left:
December 1988, Lockerbie, Scotland
Fragments of the Pan Am Boeing 747, victim
of a terrorist's bomb
© HO/Reuters

April 1, 1986, Kennedy Space Center, Florida, United States
Wreckage from the American space shuttle Challenger
in examination to determine the cause of the shuttle's explosion.
Manned space flight programmes were stopped
for more than two years
© AFP/NASA

The countdown...

January 28, 1986
Kennedy Space Center, Florida, United States
72 seconds after lift-off, the beginning of the explosion
of the rocket booster of the American space shuttle
Challenger: crew of 7 killed
© AFP/NASA

Reconstructing the catastrophe

April 1, 1986, Kennedy Space Center, Florida, United States
Wreckage from the American space shuttle Challenger in examination
to determine the cause of the shuttle's explosion. Manned space
flight programmes were stopped for more than two years
© AFP/NASA

A fateful sign in the sky

January 28, 1986, Kennedy Space Center, Florida, United States
Explosion of the American space shuttle Challenger
© Cosmos/Contact/The Orlando Sentinel

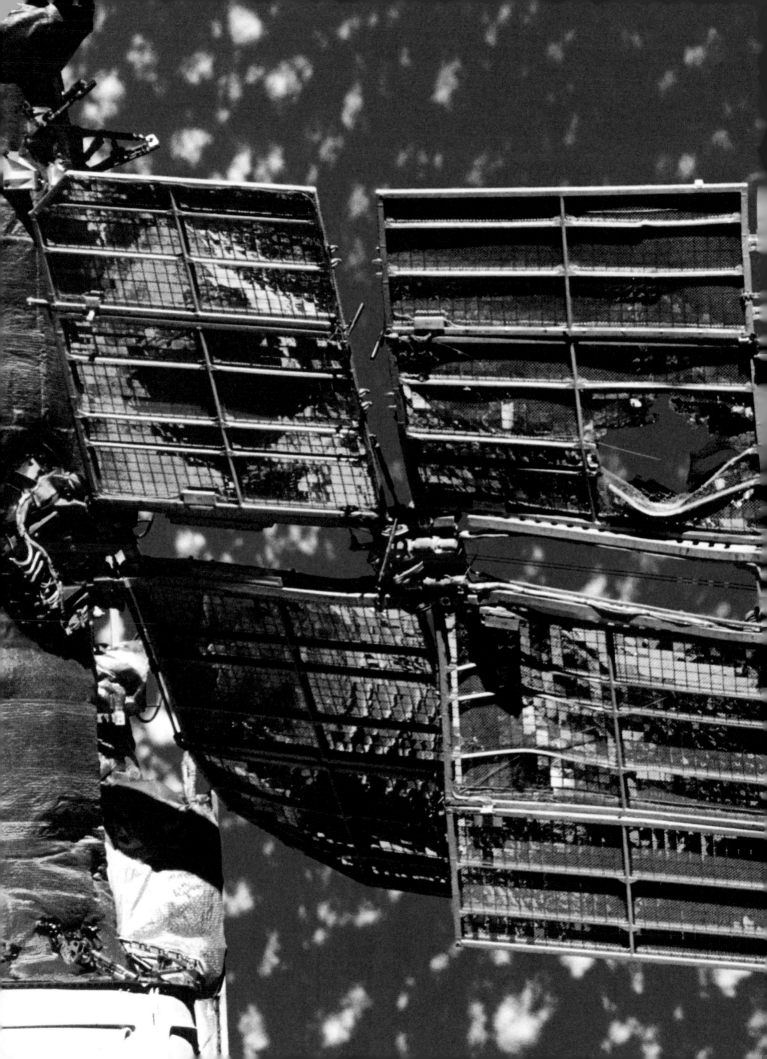

Albuquerque, New-Mexico, United States
Electrical charges being emitted by the Z machine,
the world's most powerful X-ray generator
© AFP/Sandia National Laboratories/Randy Montoya

Magnetic Fields

Preceding pages:
October 5, 1997, exterior of the Mir space station
Solar panels of the Russian space station Mir damaged
by debris orbiting the Earth
© AFP/NASA

Following pages:
1973, Amazonia, Brazil
One of the first Panará Indians to encounter
a team of researchers
© Pedro Martinelli

March 7, 1995, Tokyo, Japan
Exhausted foreign currency dealers taking a quick nap
after the dollar drops sharply in the New York
and Tokyo stock markets
AFP/Toru Yamanaka

The trauma of recognition

The unknown quantity

Paul Virilio

"Chance resembles us," wrote Bernanos and indeed if life was, in the past, still a theatre, a stage with its changing backdrops, daily life today has become pure chance, a permanent accident, with its multiple twists and turns, the spectacle of which is constantly inflicted on us from our screens.

In fact, the accident has suddenly become inhabitable, to the detriment of the substance of the shared world… This is what is meant by the "integral accident," the accident which integrates us globally, and which sometimes even disintegrates us physically. So, in a world which is now foreclosed, where all is explained by mathematics or psychoanalysis, the accident is what remains unexpected, truly surprising, the unknown quantity in a totally discovered planetary habitat, a habitat over-exposed to everyone's gaze, from which the "exotic" has suddenly disappeared in favour of that "endotic" Victor Hugo called upon when he explained to us that, "It is inside of ourselves that we have to see the outside—a terrible admission of asphyxia."[1]

"Originally," wrote Freud, "the ego includes everything, later it separates off an external world from itself. Our present ego-feeling is, therefore, only a shrunken residue of a much more inclusive—indeed, an all-embracing—feeling."[2]

Originally, Freud may be right, but in the end—and we are at the end ecologically—when our feeling is once again all-embracing by dint of the *temporal compression* of sensations, woe betide us, for we shall then be in the *great confinement*, with the once "oceanic" sense of the world incarcerated in a tiny space and, all of a sudden, claustrophobically stifled.

And this is indeed what astrophysics notes bitterly: "The break with the span of great cosmic events is one of the causes of the disorder of human societies."[3]

As evidence of this *astronomical* fracture of globalisation, let us note here an eccentric pollution phenomenon, brought to light—which is surely the *mot juste*—by a *Committee for the Protection of the Night-Skies*.

Because of the degree of light pollution created by excessively powerful electric lighting, two-thirds of humanity are now deprived of true night. On the European continent, for example, half the population are no longer able to see the Milky Way, and only the desert regions of our planet are still plunged into darkness—to the point where it is no longer merely the night sky that is threatened, but indeed the night, the great intersidereal night, that other unknown quantity which constitutes our only window on the cosmos[4]. The situation is indeed such that the International Dark-Sky Association has just launched a surrealistic petition for *the night to be listed as a part of humanity's historic heritage*!

"The World is deeper than the Day thinks," wrote Nietzsche at a time when the only light in question was still that of the sun. But already, here and there—and often even everywhere at once—contemplation of the *screen* no longer merely replaces that of the *written document*, the writing of history, but also that of the stars, to the point where the audiovisual continuum actually supplants the substantial continuum of astronomy.

In this "writing of the disaster" of space-time, in which the world becomes accessible in *real time*, humanity falls victim to myopia, reduced to the sudden foreclosure of a confinement created by the time accident of instantaneous telecommunications. From this point on, to *inhabit the integral accident* of globalisation is to asphyxiate not only *sight*, as desired by Abel Gance and later by cinemascope's advocates among film-makers, but the daily *life* of a species endowed, for all that, with the movement of being.

At this stage of incarceration, terminal history becomes a process running behind closed doors, as was so well explained by the inmates of the concentration camps: "Our horror, our stupor, is our lucidity."[5]

Everything is there, already there, *déjà-vu* and soon even *déjà-dit*, already-said. All that remains then is the waiting, the long waiting for a *catastrophic* horizon that will succeed the *geographical* horizon of the round Earth.

So, the *local* accident situated here or there gives way to the great accident, the *global* accident which integrates by turns all the setbacks and hitches that formerly characterized societal life, to the point where this "great confinement" puts an end to banishment and exclusion, in favour, entirely, of causal chains, since now, "Everything arrives without it being necessary to depart," to move towards the other, the wholly other—as in the past one moved towards the horizontal limit of a landscape.

Here, *pace* Nietzsche, it is no longer God the Father who dies, but the Earth, the Mother of living creatures since the dawn of time.

With light and the speed of light, *it is the whole of matter that is exterminated*. The telluric accident of the earthquake gives way to the seism of a timequake, of that *global time* that eliminates all distance.

In the sudden telescoping of successive events that have become simultaneous, it is *extension* and *duration* that are swept away.

After first been shattered by the nuclear bomb, matter is now exterminated by acceleration, the specular bomb of screens, these mirrors of time, which blot out the horizon.

In the enclosure of its terrestrial environment, reaching the threshold of an intersidereal void which humanity has by no means conquered and indeed dreads, "the limit experience is the experience of what there is 'outside of everything,' when the everything excludes any outside."[6]

At this culminating point, as we arrive at the twenty-first century, what is heralded is not so much the end of history as the end of multiple time-scales. Suddenly, with the extermination of the distances of the *local time* of geophysics, and faced with the light years of a purely astrophysical time, "Mankind has, in a sense, gathered at the Omega point, which means there is no longer any other than mankind and that there is no longer any outside outside of him."[7]

The ultimate figure of philanoia,[8] that is to say, of the knowledge accident in which, "Mankind, affirming everything by his very existence, understands everything by understanding itself in the closed circle of knowledge."[9]

Then, within the limits of this closure, something excessive lies in waiting—not, as in the "*exile* of madness" of the deviants the eighteenth century confined in asylums, but in the *exodus* of the powerful's love of madness—these mad scientists stigmatized by Jonathan Swift, rendered impotent by the obsessional excess of discoveries which are not so much sub-human as profoundly inhuman.

And how, other than as a major clinical symptom, can we interpret the fact that more than ten million people in France today indulge in the mania for video games, frequenting the networked games sites as one might an opium den, connecting to the Internet in the way one might get one's fix of a drug?

The vogue for "on-line games", a panic phenomenon of dependence, has lent a new dimension to what psychiatry terms de-realization, carrying adults and adolescents off to an insubstantial *parallel world*, where everyone gradually adjusts to **inhabiting the accident** of an audiovisual continuum independent of the real space of one's life. At this stage of a cybernetic confinement that is presented as an achievement of Progress, when the slightest item of information and the tiniest event speed around the world in an instant, globalisation puts an end to "revolution" as it does to classical "world war" since, thanks to televisual ubiquity, the slightest incident can become "revolutionary" and the tiniest attack, when looped around, can assume the gigantic proportions of a world conflict!

The effect of this **Omega** point reached by humanity is finally here—a "meteorological" effect which reproduces the effect of the butterfly's wings in Asia that creates a hurricane in Europe, the way the *El Niño* phenomenon is currently causing upheaval in the global climate.

In this sense, as Maurice Blanchot indicated, writing of the Enlightenment, "To enclose the outside, that is to say, to constitute it as **interiority** of expectation or exception— such is the exigency which leads society to make madness exist or, in other words, to make it possible." [10]

This is what is happening to our globalised societies, in which the *local* is the outside and the *global* the inside of a finished world, defined solely by the networks of instantaneous information and communication, to the detriment of any "geopolitics", since the **real time** of (economic, political etc.) exchanges is winning out definitively over the **real space** of the geophysics of the regions of the world.

I*n accelerating, globalisation is turning the world inside out like a glove*— from now on, the near is foreign and the exotic close at hand.

The deregulation of transport has given way to the *dérèglement* of a **foreclosure** that prompts the **exclusion** of "the near and the neighbouring" in favour, momentarily, of any "distant thing or person" encountered in the chance concertinaing of civilizations. The horizons of expectation of a three-centuries-old past that is now dead and gone give way to anxious expectation of the *Great* (eco-eschatological) *Accident*, of which industrial accidents and terrorist attacks are only ever a foreshadowing, the symptoms of a complete turnabout in the orientation of humanity.

But this latest of all expectations is inseparable from the *time accident*,[11] since the acquisition of light-speed unifies social timescales and promotes a generalized syn-chronization of action, with interactivity now supplanting plain activity. Remote action—teleaction—which eliminates not just the long run of family and social relations, but also that of the political economy of nations and their military strategies.

Hence this recent overthrow of *substantial* (or, Clausewitzian) *warfare* in favour of *accidental war* which, being anonymous and profoundly random, marries declared hostilities with industrial or other accidents, promoting a fatal confusion between accidents and attacks.

Global terrorism, in fact, resembles Destiny and its "strokes of fate", the *force of destiny* putting the final touch to the force of classical armies, equipped with weapons of mass destruction inherited from an era of world war that is now past and gone. But Victor Hugo writes: "I have defined and delimited the 'state of emergency': if anarchy is arbitrariness in the street, arbitrary rule is the anarchy of power."[12]

Henceforth, globalisation provides the "state of emergency", that foreclosure which transforms, or will soon transform, every state into a *police state*, every army into *a police force* and every community into a *ghetto*…

The effect of the closed field of globalisation is, then, simply the progressive asphyxia of the constitutional state of representative democracy, with "control society" replacing the society of local confinement. After the standardization that came out of the industrial revolution, synchronization (both of opinion and decision-making) represents an ultimate model of tyranny: the tyranny of this real time of a forced interaction which is replacing the real space of action, and free reaction to it, within the extended realm of an open world.

If interactivity is to information what radioactivity is to matter—namely, a power of contamination and disintegration—then the integral time accident combines the deflagrations of the socius and of its intelligibility, gradually rendering the whole world opaque. After the accident befalling substances—the material accident—the time of the knowledge accident is here. This is what cybernetics is: the arbitrariness of anarchy in the power of nations, the various powers of a community not simply *made idle* by auto-mation, but *unhinged* by the sudden synchronization of human activities.

Notes

1. Victor Hugo, *Things Seen: Choses vues* (Seattle: University Press of the Pacific, 2001).

2. Sigmund Freud, "Civilization and its Discontents," *Civilization, Society and Religion* (London: Penguin, 'Penguin Freud Library', vol. 12, 1991).

3. Sylvie Vauclair, *La chanson du soleil* (Paris: Éditions Albin Michel, 2002).

4. "Une loi pour sauver la nuit" (*Le Figaro*, June 3, 2002).

5. Robert Antelme, *The Human Race* (Evanston: Northwestern University Press, 1998).

6. Maurice Blanchot, *The Infinite Conversation* (Minneapolis : Minnesota University Press, 1993).

7. *Op. cit.*

8. *Philofolie*: love of madness.

9. *Op. cit.*

10. *Op. cit.*

11. "Time is the accident of accidents," Aristotle, *Physics*.

12. Victor Hugo, *op.cit.*

Text translated from French by Chris Turner

Bibliography

François-Xavier Albouy, *Le temps des catastrophes*
(Paris: Éditions Descartes et Cie, 2002)

Svetlana Aleksievich, *Voices from Chernobyl: Chronicle of the Future*
(London: Aurum Press, 1990)

Hannah Arendt, *The Origins of Totalitarianism* (London: André Deutsch, 1968)

Aristotle, *Physics, Books I-IV* (London: Heinemann, 'Loeb Classical Library', 1929)

Henri Atlan, *La Science est-elle inhumaine?*
(Paris: Éditions Bayard Centurion, collection 'Temps d'une Question', 2002)

Jacques Attali, *Économie de l'Apocalypse* (Paris: Éditions Fayard, 1995)

Maurice Blanchot, *The Infinite Conversation*
(Minneapolis: Minnesota University Press, 1993)

Albert Camus, *Réflexions sur le terrorisme* (Paris: Éditions Nicolas Philippe, 2002)

Ben Cramer, *Le Nucléaire dans tous ses états* (Paris: Éditions Alias, 2002)

Jean-Pierre Dupuy, *Pour un catastrophisme éclairé* (Paris: Éditions du Seuil, 2002)

Jacques Ellul, *The Technological Bluff*
(Grand Rapids, Michigan: Wm. B. Eerdmans Publishing Co., 1998)

Sigmund Freud, 'Civilization and its Discontents', *Civilization, Society and Religion*
(London: Penguin, 'Penguin Freud Library' vol. 12, 1991)

Brigitte Friang, *Regarde-toi qui meurs* (Paris: Éditions du Félin, 1997)

Jean Gimpel, *The End of the Future* (London: Adamantine Press, 1995)

Günter Grass, *Crabwalk* (Orlando, Florida: Harcourt Brace, forthcoming, April 2003)

Armand Hatchuel *et al.*, *Experts in Organizations* (Berlin: Walter de Gruyter, 1995)

Victor Hugo, *Things Seen: Choses vues* (Seattle: University Press of the Pacific, 2001)

Hans Jonas, *The Imperative of Responsibility*
(Chicago: University of Chicago Press, 1984)

Karl Kraus, *In These Great Times* (Manchester: Carcanet, 1984)

Patrick Lagadec, *Major Technological Risk* (Oxford: Pergamon Press, 1982)

Patrick Mauriès, *Les Cabinets de curiosité* (Paris: Éditions Gallimard, 2002)

Théodore Monod, *Sortie de secours* (Paris: Éditions Seghers, 1991)

Christian Morel, *Les Décisions absurdes* (Paris: Éditions Gallimard, 2002)

Friedrich Nietzsche, *The Birth of Tragedy and other writings*
(Cambridge: Cambridge University Press, 1999)

René Passet, *Mondialisation financière et terrorisme*
(Paris: Éditions de l'Atelier, collection 'Enjeux Planète', 2002)

Antoine Picon, *La Ville et la guerre* (Paris: Éditions de l'Imprimeur, 1996)

Léon Poliakov, *La Causalité diabolique* (Paris: Éditions Calmann-Lévy, 1980)

Hermann Rauschning, *Germany's Revolution of Destruction*
(London: Heinemann, 1939)

Jérôme Sgard, *L'économie de la panique* (Paris: Éditions La Découverte, 2002)

Joseph E. Stiglitz, *Globalization and its Discontents* (London: Allen Lane, 2002)

Paul Valéry, 'La Crise de l'intelligence', *Œuvres complètes*, vol. I
(Paris: Éditions Gallimard, collection 'Bibliothèque de la Pléiade', 1957)

Renaud Vié-Lesage, *La Terre en otage* (Paris: Éditions du Seuil, 1989)

Paul Virilio, *Politics of the Very Worst* (New York: Semiotext(e), 1998)

Paul Virilio, *A Landscape of Events* (London/Cambridge, Mass.: MIT Press, 2000)

Paul Virilio, *Ground Zero* (London: Verso, 2002)

Norbert Wiener, *God and Golem Inc.* (London/Cambridge, Mass: MIT Press, 1964)

'Accident, Catastrophe', in *Confrontations*, n° 7, 1982

Philips Galle,
Disaster of the Hebrew people, the destruction of the Tower of Babel, 1569
Engraving after Martin van Heemskerck

4

March 3, 1989, Lille, France
Destruction by implosion of an 18-story council flat building
© AFP/Boris Horvat

October 11, 1994, Venissieux, Rhône, France
Most important implosion ever performed in France:
6 blocks of council flats demolished
© AFP/Gérard Malie

Implosion or explosion?

October 24, 1998, Detroit, United States
Tallest building ever imploded:
2.2 million square feet standing at 410 feet,
25 floors and four basements,
2,728 pounds of explosives,
660 million pounds of rubble and
6 months of clean-up
© AFP/Jeff Kowalsky

April 19, 1995, Oklahoma City, Oklahoma, United States
North side of the Albert P. Murrah Federal Building devastated by
a fuel and fertilizer bomb: 168 people killed and more than 500 injured
© AFP/Bob Daemmrich

September 11, 2001, New York, United States
The south tower of the World Trade Center begins to collapse
following the attack by terrorist-controlled airliners,
and subsequent fire: about 2,800 people killed

Hurtling debris during the collapse
of the World Trade Center's
south tower
© AFP/Wirepix/Jim Sulley

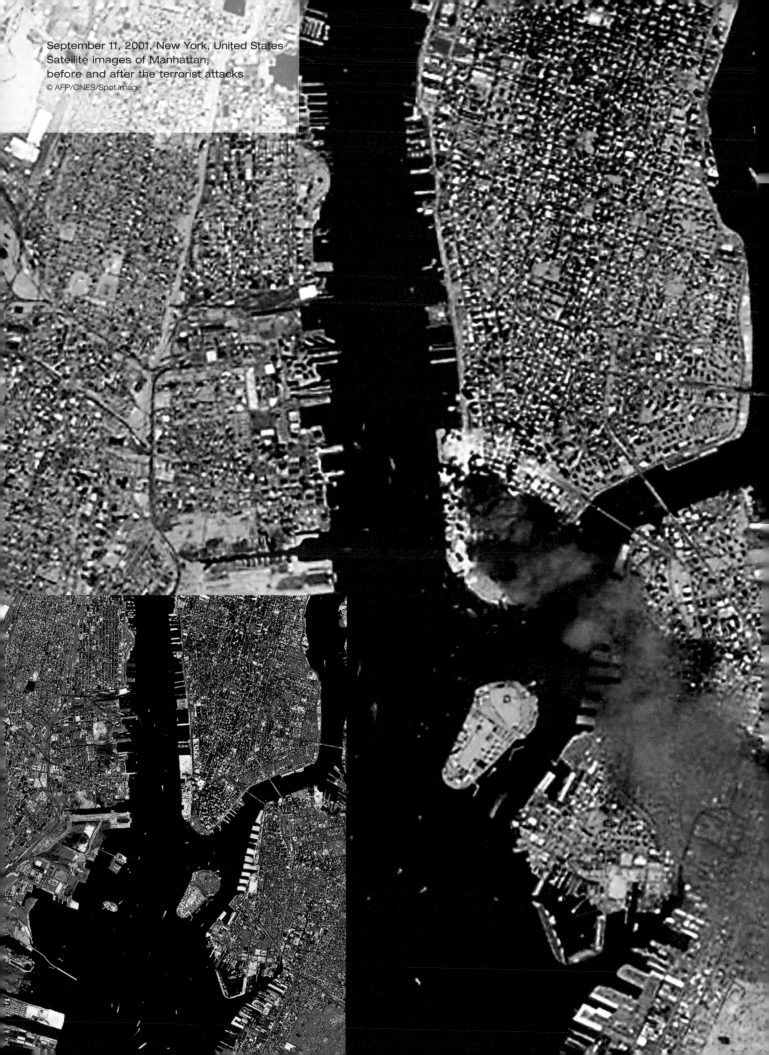

September 11, 2001, New York, United States
Satellite images of Manhattan,
before and after the terrorist attacks
© AFP/CNES/Spot Image

September 12, 2001, Washigton DC, United States
Satellite image of the Pentagon
after the terrorist attack against the west wing
of the building, September 11, 2001
© Space Imaging/Sipa

Following page:
September 14, 2001
New York, United States
Ruins of the World Trade Center
© AFP/Navy Visual News Service/Jim Watson

Lebbeus Woods

Stephen Vitiello

Nancy Rubins

The Fall
Lebbeus Woods

September 23, 2001, New York, United States
Aerial photo of Manhattan as smoke rises from the ruins
of the World Trade Center
© AFP Cessna Citation Jet/NOAA

The whole enterprise of architecture is so heavily invested in the idea of resisting gravity that even the thought of a building falling down before its time is nothing short of a nightmare scenario. The heroic works of architecture are those that lift the materials of a building higher, or extend them farther, or make them thinner, or fashion a new form that defies gravity's dominion and pushes the envelope of what is thought possible. It is one thing to plan a building's demolition, when it is deemed to have outlived its usefulness, quite another when it falls unexpectedly, while it is still a viable structure for living and work. In such a case, there is not only a sudden loss of property, and of pride and confidence, but almost always of human lives. This traumatic scenario is played out every time a major earthquake occurs in a heavily built-up and populated urban area, bringing down scores of buildings that injure or kill thousands. It occurs when fire breaks out in a building and trapped inhabitants die from smoke and flames and heat. It occurs when neglect or 'deferred maintenance' allow structural weaknesses of a building to grow into catastrophic failures. It occurs when war flares up in some part of the world and buildings blasted by bombs and artillery shells become death chambers rather than the sanctuaries they were intended to be. It occurred in Oklahoma City, when an American terrorist's bomb brought down the Federal Building, and in New York, when the World Trade Center towers fell under the aerial attack of Islamic extremists.

The consequences of this attack and the fall of the towers have been global in their scope and apocalyptic in their intensity. The United States government has dedicated billions to the erection of a 'homeland' defense bureaucracy intended to stop future suicide bombers from fulfilling their desperately holy mission of destruction. It has also suspended some long-standing legal protections against unreasonable searches, seizures, detentions, surveillance, ensuring the advent of a new era of political crimes and secret police presence in many aspects of formerly private life. Other governments around the world, fearing that their 'motherlands' or 'fatherlands' will be the next targets, are following suit, which bodes ill for the future of democracy everywhere, but especially in those countries where it has little or no hold already. Not least, vast new sums have been dedicated to military budgets, diverting resources and attention from badly needed social programs.

Given all this, it is strange indeed that the response of architects has been so routine. With one of the most urgently complex events in recent history unfolding before them, they have busied themselves with making designs for new buildings of various sorts for the WTC site, dutifully living up to their job descriptions, and at the same time exposing a bankruptcy of critical faculties, not to mention imagination. Because their chosen field is so comprehensive, incorporating aspects of science, art, politics, economics and the rest of a long list of human concerns, one would expect them to look deeper into the event and its aftermath than, say, politicians or stock brokers or physicians. Because architecture is at the very center of the event and the broad range of controversies around it, one would expect them to feel the weight of their special responsibility to cast a long and critical eye on the complex role architecture played in it, as prelude to any proposals for rebuilding. It hasn't happened.

Understandably, the first reaction of people and their institutions to catastrophes of this order is to fix the blame on the particular forces of nature that brought about the destruction, or the particular national enemies, or the perpetrators of the crime. Considering the need for defense against possible and imminent recurrences we naturally look for the most immediate and direct cause of the fall and of its disastrous consequences. Blame is fixed and measures taken. Everyone waits for the next blow. If it does not come we assume that the measures taken were an effective remedy. This is reasonable only if we do not consider them first aid applied to a traumatic wound. The break in the surface is closed, the bleeding stops, healing—at least at the surface—begins. The deeper wound, the trauma itself, embodied in the fall and its memory, is examined only in medical and academic quarters far from public forums and discussion.

So abhorrent is the idea of the fall, so quick the rush to erase its evidence, so single-minded the effort to rebuild the sameness, that the reality of the fall itself and the nature of the transformations it has brought about are obscured. It is no surprise, then, that there is no progress in dealing with the unexpected fall of buildings. What is offered instead is a ritual re-enactment of 'the primordial fall.' The same shock, the same platitudes uttered by the same people, the same search for villains, for heroes, for quick and effective remedies: the same desire to restore normalcy, even though it was that very normalcy which sponsored the catastrophic event. Considering the tremendous capacity of human beings to penetrate complex phenomena and explicate their innermost workings—the atomic structure of matter, the workings of the human

153

aftermath of catastrophe, it is only effects that are strenuously addressed. While this neatly sets the stage for the next re-enactment, with all its cathartic potential, an opportunity to embrace events more fully and to act more creatively is missed. It should be the purpose of experimental works of art and architecture to explore and reveal what T. S. Eliot called the Shadow that falls between the idea and the act, the obscured realm between cause and effect—the space of the fall itself.

The installation designed for the main exhibition space of Jean Nouvel's lucid building for the Fondation Cartier is entitled *The Fall*. Its ambition is to expose the fall as a micro-universe that crystallizes the dimensions of a precise, if abbreviated, moment. In the space measuring roughly 53 feet by 66 feet by 25 feet high, enclosed on three sides by floor to ceiling glass, a particular construction has been made, a physical and at the same time hypothetical manifestation of the fall.

Let us say, for the purposes of understanding the hypothesis, that the exhibition space suddenly collapses, as the ceiling falls down toward the floor. This fall may be the product of any number of different causes—structural defects in construction or design, a terrorist's bomb exploding, or something else entirely unexpected. The structural system, the materials supporting the building, resisting the imperative to fall, succumb to the attraction of gravity, suddenly giving way, precipitating a fall toward the planet's center of mass. Gravity is nothing more nor less than acceleration, induced by the attraction of masses. In this case, the attraction is manifest at 32 feet per second. In the first second, the ceiling of the exhibition space falls 16 feet towards the floor. After the next second, it would be some 25 feet

psyche, the evolutionary histories of extinct forms of life—one begins to suspect that when it comes to catastrophes like the unexpected fall of buildings, intellectual and emotional regression sets in. Confronted with the spectacle of something perfectly whole and stable, a coherent human presence within, that becomes—a moment later—a pile of smoking rubble, in which the human presence has been extinguished, imagination quails, reverting to formulas of magic and superstition.

In the mythical, black and white universe of good and evil, of hero and villain, there is only before and after. Thus, the fall affects everything, but changes nothing. Trauma and tragedy reveal only never completely connectable causes and effects. In such a universe, causes are reduced to easily digested stereotypes and inevitably put aside. In the long

154 below the floor, well into the buildings many basements. The ceiling structures of the basements slow down the buildings fall, as the upper floors meet the resistance of the subterranean structure. Still, the collapse of the exhibition space takes less than two seconds. Too fast to see, no doubt, but not at all too fast to conceptualize. This is the time-space of the fall—too brief to inhabit—except in imagination.

The essential feature of the fall is the acceleration of mass resulting from the disturbance of the inertia of the upper building masses by some external force. There is a tremendous release of energy, the 'potential' stored in the materials and their arrangement above the ground that became 'kinetic' when they were liberated by a disturbance outside their system. Tremendous sound, dust, calamity. But what about the space? What happens to the space?

In the absence of actual collapse, we can project. The building's spatial system—a rectilinear 3-D grid—descends. The space of the exhibition is filled. It becomes a volume, in this case not of fallen materials but of trajectories. The rectilinear system of ordering the spaces of the building is projected downward, toward the ground and below, toward the center of the earth. The fall of the grid would be straight if it were unimpeded, but there are perturbances in the active forces, irregularities in the grid that are amplified by the external forces, resistances encountered on the way down, as well as accidental collisions between descending vectors. The resulting spatial distortion is evident in the cumulative configuration of trajectory lines. In their descent, the downward trajectories of the grid have become idiosyncratic. There has been an interaction between their vectors, producing gaps, distances, dimensions that effectively form new and unexpected spaces within the former system. In falling, a transformation occurs. The former, regular order of spatial organization becomes 'irregular,' or regular in ways unaccounted for by the former system.

This new spatial organization is a territory wide open for speculation. We can safely suppose that it is based not on stability but on instability, on change, literally, the change of one form into another, perhaps even of one language of form into another language. The former case is self-evident—we need only look. The latter case is true only if the rules governing language and its use have been transformed. And indeed they have—we need only think. Just as the physical structure acted upon by physical forces external to the system has 'deformed,' or 'reformed,' into a new configuration, so the strictly deterministic 'rule structure' of the rectilinear grid has been acted upon by the force of unanticipated, non-deterministic events, reforming it, too, into a new type of structure that engages the unpredictable conditions created by sudden and unexpected change.

Paul Virilio's insight that the accidents occurring within a system are as designed as its intended results corresponds closely with the dynamics of unpredictability characteristic of a culture based on innovation and technological progress. As this implies, determinism by itself is no longer an adequate framework for understanding contemporary life or spaces designed for it, yet we cannot dispense with it. Instead, we should seek to enlarge its scope and deepen its implications. Determinism must be wedded, as it were, to non-determinism. Goal-oriented predictability must be expanded to embrace accidents, chance, randomness, unpredictability. This as we know has already happened in physics, biology, cognitive science. It has happened in art to a more limited extent. It has happened in the everyday for people living in the technologically advanced countries, whose jobs and futures are dependent upon emotion-driven fluctuations in stock-markets, currency speculation, and the vicissitudes of international politics. But it has not yet happened in architecture and design. True, there have been premonitory rumblings in the attempts by some architects to integrate post-modern concepts such as 'deconstruction' into their practices, and by others trying to use computer technology to generate new forms and processes of formation, but these seem tentative at best—even this avant-garde for the most part remains loyal to traditional ideas of what a building "wants to be."

When design aims only at enabling a desired stability—social, economic, psychological—the goals are determined in advance. A space is deemed 'functional,' if it can be used in the way the designer prescribed and, presumably, its client or anticipated users intended. But when, as is often the case today, the goal is to enable unpredictability, to give people a high degree of freedom in how and why they need or use designed space, it is no longer possible to think of function, or purpose, or meaning as we have before. Mere 'flexibility,' in the old sense of adapting a form designed for one purpose to another purpose, or the same form to a variety of purposes, misses the point. What is needed are entirely new ways of thinking and working. The fall instructs us as to what these need to be.

Accidents, in the deterministic sense, are not designed, but simply 'happen.' They are out of control in that we can never predict exactly what, where or when. But they are designed, in the Virilian sense, because the creation of any working system insures their probability, thus their inevitability. In that sense, we had better learn how to live with them, if they are not always to be catastrophic, or to work creatively with them, if anything constructive is to emerge in their aftermath. The first step is to acknowledge that accidents arise spontaneously not from an infinite number of possibilities, but from a limited set of probabilities: a matrix, a trajectory field of unpredictably transforming vectors. They arise, in this case, from *within* the fall itself.

The fall, if we look closely and think critically, is a hybrid. It is a transformation, embracing at least two systems, one changing into the other. A process and a philosophy, the fall is a becoming, and a paradox, because it is two different, even opposing, things at the same time.

So, too with the installation. Pre-determined design goals are combined with spontaneous invention according to new types of rules for the shaping of space activated in the course of the installation process. The architect is no longer the planner who determines the shape of space in advance, but one who sets up the limits—the rule structure of materials and how they are shaped—then steps back and lets collaborators do the work. Design as a determination in advance of what is to happen and how is brought together with design as a calculated risk, an acceptance of accidents within a set of declared limits. In the fall, if we are open enough to perceive it, we discover that not only the forms of designed space are changed, but also the nature of how, even why, we design. In the process we find that we, too, have been transformed, and will never see the world again in the same way.

While the space of the fall isn't for everyone, it is part of an emerging reality few will be able to avoid or escape. It is an experimental domain where limits of all kinds are tested for those willing to take risks and embrace changes. It may be a foretaste of what is to come for a society that cares more for progress than security and values liberty above certainty. It may also be a glimpse into what architecture might become if it invests its creative capital less in the struggle against gravity and more in seeing what might happen when we let go.

Fondation Cartier pour l'art contemporain, Paris
Jean Nouvel, architect
Photo P. Gries

New York City, July 14, 2002

Lebbeus Woods
The Fall, 2002
Concept and design: Lebbeus Woods
With the collaboration of Alexis Rochas
Courtesy Henry Urbach Architecture, New York
© 2002 by Lebbeus Woods

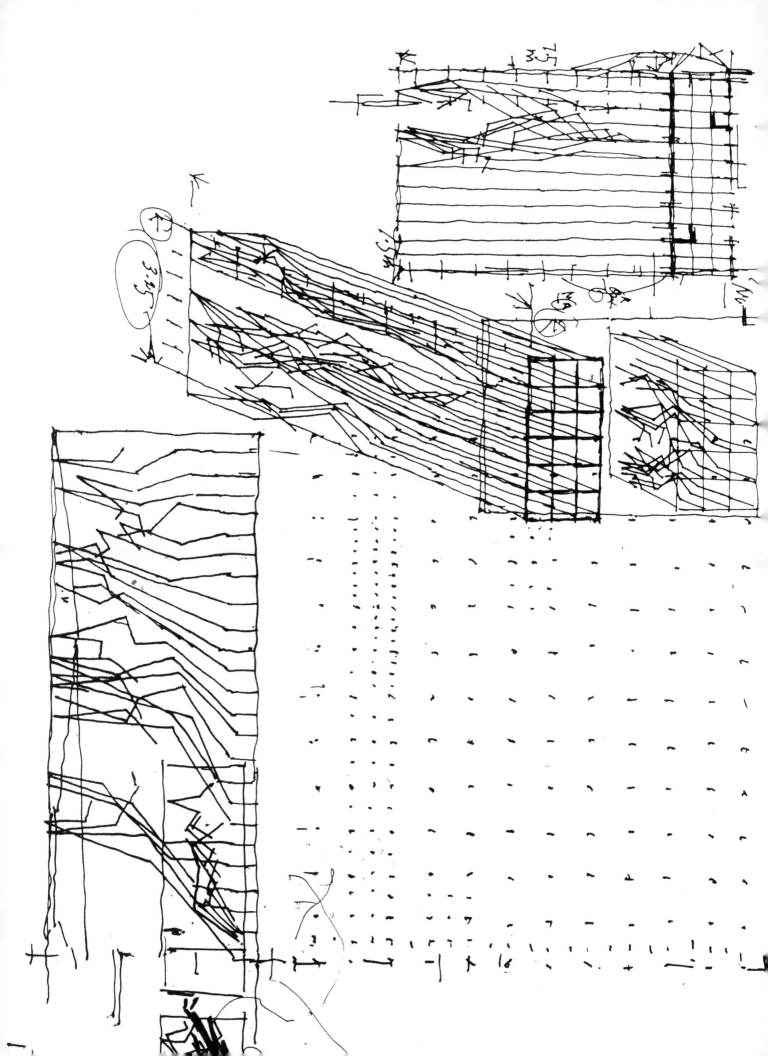

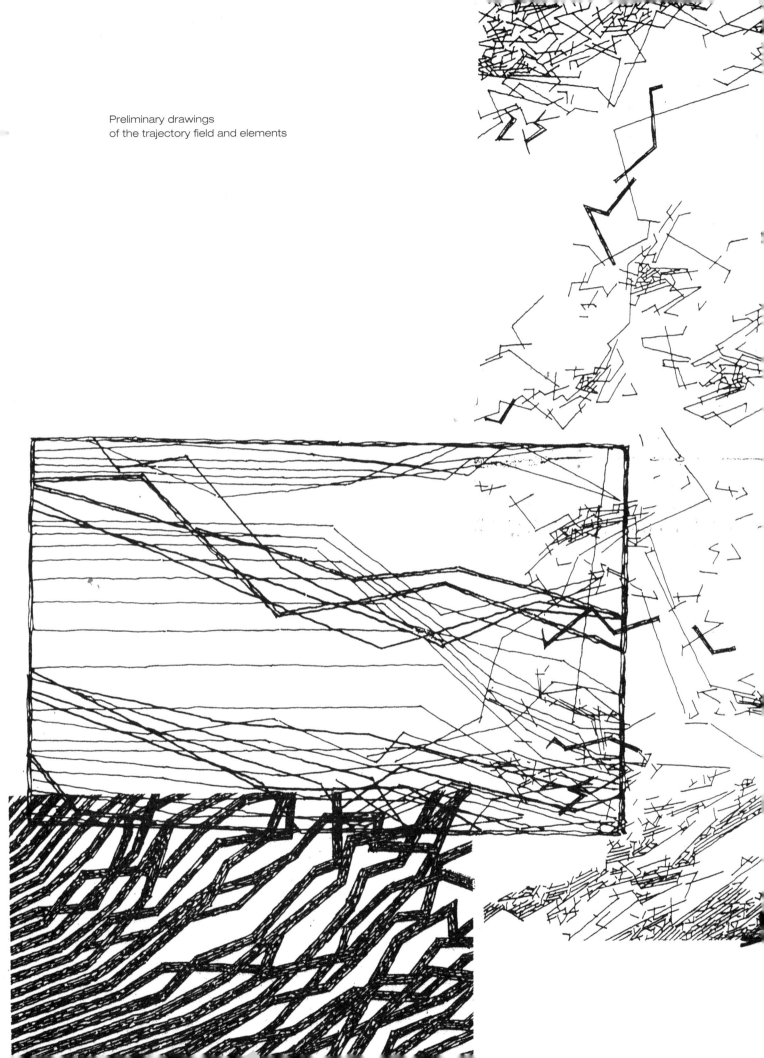

Preliminary drawings
of the trajectory field and elements

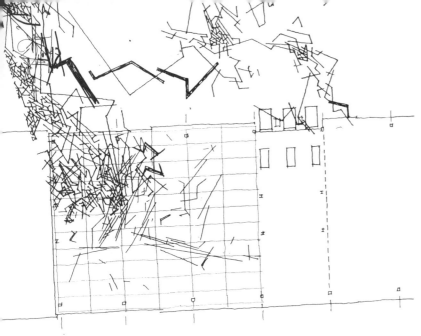

Preliminary drawing of the trajectory field and elements

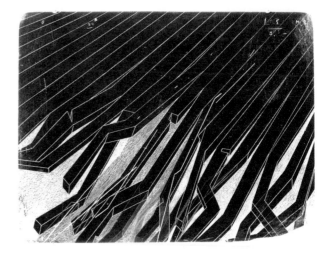

View of suspension field elements

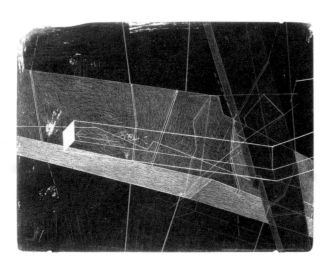

Detail of suspended elements

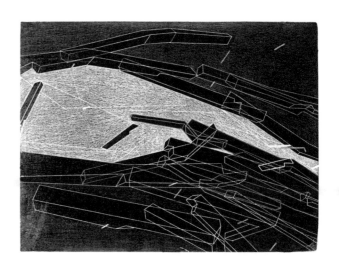

View of suspension field and elements

View of debris field

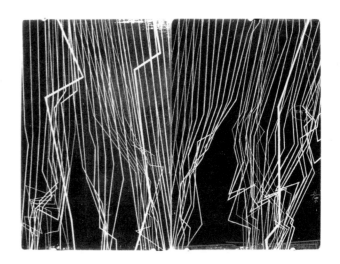

Elevations of vectors in trajectory field

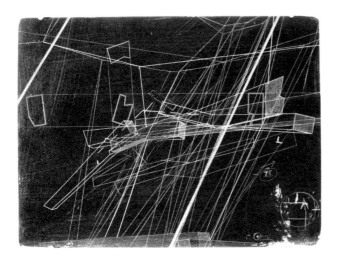

View of suspension field, wires, elements

Detail of suspended elements

View of suspension field and elements

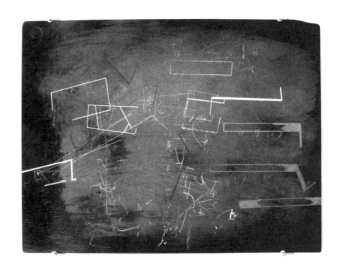

View of debris field

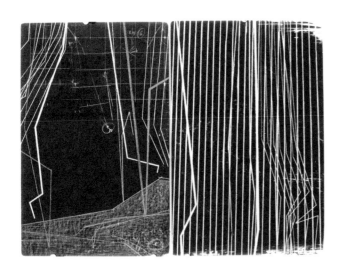

Elevations of vectors in trajectory field

Axonometric view of grid and vectors
in trajectory field

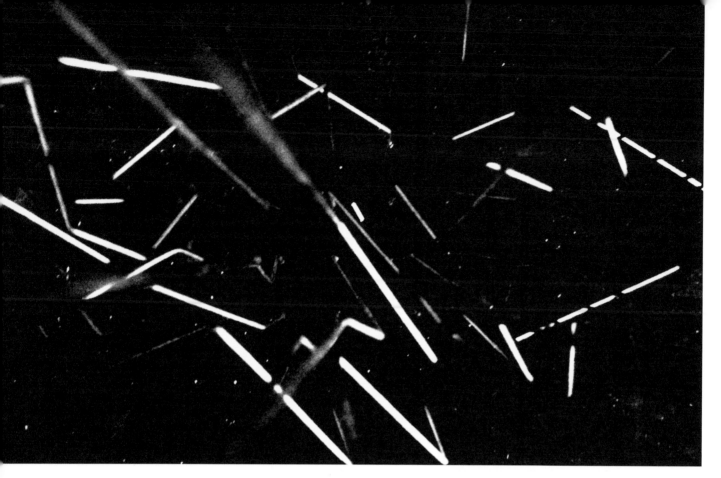

Partial reflected view within trajectory field (model)

Elevation of trajectory field (model)

Reflected view of trajectory field (model)

View within trajectory field (model)

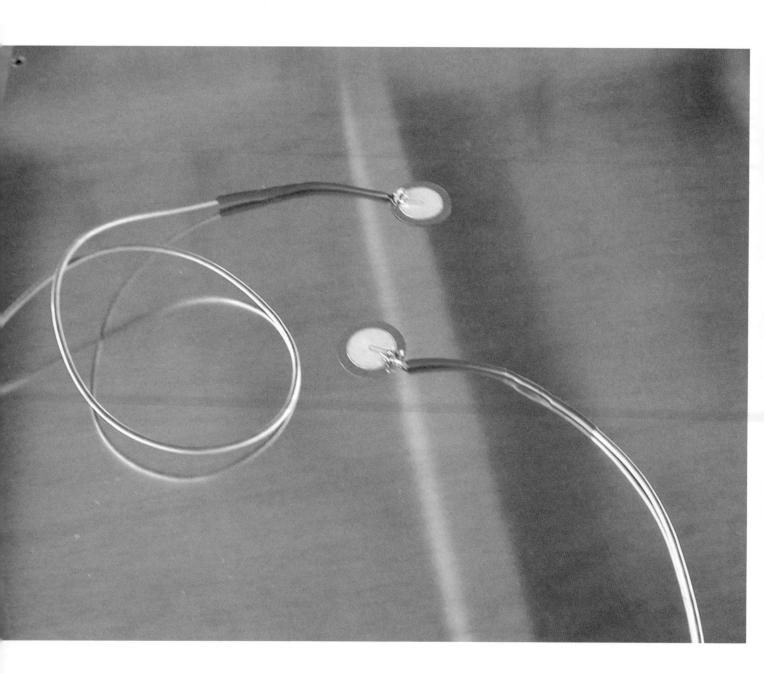

Stephen Vitiello
Listening to Judd, 2002
Sound recording: contact microphones picking up sound vibration
through Donald Judd's sculptures
Unauthorized recording, Chinati, Marfa, Texas

Contact microphones on Steel Plate, Chinati, 2002
Sound recording

Nancy Rubins
MoMA & Airplane Parts, 1995
Mixed media
Dimensions: variable
Courtesy of the artist and Gagosian Gallery
Photo: Adam Reich
© 1995 Nancy Rubins

Dominic Angerame

In the Course of Human Events, 1997

16 mm, black and white

Duration: 23.5 min

Directed, filmed and edited by Dominic Angerame © 1997

Sound Design: Amy Leigh Hunter

Music: Kevin Barnard © 1997

Additional Music: "Wiltshire Mix", Ray Guillett & Bond Bergland ©1997

Electric Bass by Kyle Newell

Nine-Eleven

Tony Oursler
Nine-Eleven, 2001
Mini-DV Digital Video
Duration: approx. 53 min
© Tony Oursler

"Everyone loves a parade,
except for the dead"

Jem Cohen
Little Flags, 2000
Super 8 film
Duration: 6 min
Music: Fugazi
(soundtrack mix by Jem Cohen and David Frankel)
Courtesy of the filmmaker © 1992/2000

Wolfgang Staehle
Untitled, 2001
Webcam
Duration: 24 hours
Real time recording of a panoramic view of Lower Manhattan,
broadcast on the Internet throughout September 2001, initiated without prior knowledge
of the events that would take place on September 11
© Wolfgang Staehle/Courtesy of Max Protetch Gallery

Cai Guo-Qiang
Tonight So Lovely, 2001/2002. Two videos from the Asia Pacific Economic Cooperation Cityscape Fireworks: Oriental Television live broa

x. 19 min) and artist's version (approx. 20 min). Courtesy of Cai Studio. © Cai Guo-Qiang

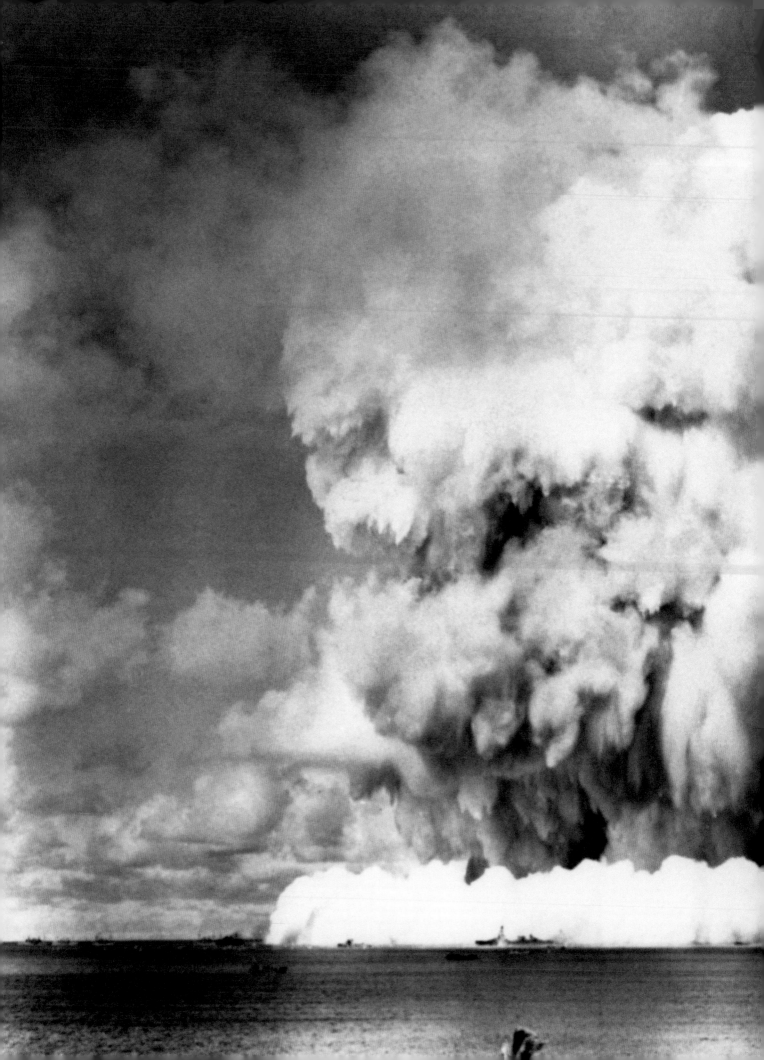

Bruce Conner

A MOVIE, 1958
16 mm, black and white
Duration : 12 min
Music: *Pini di Roma*, Ottorino Respighi
© 1958 Bruce Conner

CROSSROADS, 1976
35 mm
Duration: 36 min
Music: Patrick Gleeson and Terry Riley
© 1975 Bruce Conner
Produced with a grant from the American Film Institute

Peter Hutton
Boston Fire, 1978
16 mm black and white, silent film
Duration: 8 min
© Peter Hutton

New York Portrait: Chapter Two, 1980-1981
16 mm black and white, silent film
Duration: 15 min

Moira Tierney
American Dreams #3, 2001
16 mm
Duration: 5 min
Music: Charlemagne Palestine
Stills: Arunas Kulikauskas
© Moira Tierney 2001

"Ina's images, images
engraved in your mind"
Cinq colonnes à la une
Et maintenant Agadir, 1960
Black and white film
Duration : 18 min.
© Ina

Aernout Mik
Middlemen, 2001
Video installation
Edition of 4 + 1 a.p.
Duration: 21 min, looped
Camera: Benito Strangio
Directing Assistance: Marjoleine Boonstra
Courtesy carlier | gebauer

Ein Märchen aus alten Zeiten

Following pages:

Artavazd Achotowich Pelechian
Our Century, 1990 (short version)
35 mm
Duration: 30 min
© Artavazd Achotowich Pelechian

Jonas Mekas
Ein Märchen aus alten Zeiten, 2001
Video
Duration: 6 min
Music: Jonas Mekas
© Jonas Mekas

September 28, 2002

An interview,
Svetlana Aleksievich
and Paul Virilio
for Andrei Ujica's film
Unknown Quantity

Paul Virilio: Svetlana, what are we going to talk about? About Chernobyl?
Svetlana Aleksievich: Let's try. Let's talk about this mystery again. It's a mystery that still intrigues me at any rate, even though my book was written a long time ago.

P.V.: Chernobyl is an event totally outside the norm. It is an atypical event. It is part of what might be referred to by the term "unknown quantity". Alongside progress – that is to say, the qualitative achievements of science, there is a quantitative logic. The more intense the progress, the more catastrophic and painful the accidents, the tragedies. What was your experience of this accident at Chernobyl through meetings with the people involved, through testimony?
S.A.: I am trying to remember now the first days after the accident: how it went, how I plunged into this mystery. I remember that, at the beginning, none of the conversations about it provided any explanation. We were all confused. We would look at one another and find no words to express our emotions. Mostly, people just kept saying, "I didn't read it anywhere, I didn't see it anywhere, no-one talked to me about that." There was a colossal break with our past. That past proved powerless to help us.

P.V.: This is perhaps because it was an accident of time more than an accident of space. Accidents in the past related to space. The Titanic sank in the North Atlantic. A plane crashed at an air base. But in this case it was an accident in time, in tempo-rality. The Chernobyl event is outside the norm in the sense that it concerned astronomical time, the time of generations, centuries and millennia. It is an accident which, in this sense, is not so much attached to space and materiality as to temporality. Is this something that interested you with the people you met, this relation to time?
S.A.: It was immediately obvious—as soon as you saw people's distressed expressions—that we had been pitched into a new reality and that the layer of culture which normally protected us had shattered instantaneously. We found ourselves naked—bare people on a bare earth. We were forced to start over again from scratch. So, I tried (this is what people expected of me), I tried to put my finger on what had happened, which was beyond our ken and our imagining. Now, we were immediately confronted with the problem of our maladjustment to the event. Because the first sensation there, in the disaster zone, is that our biological machinery is not adapted to this. We, God's creatures, are not ready for it: our eyes can't see radiation, our noses can't smell it, our hands can't touch it. Our biology isn't prepared for it. And our vocabulary isn't adapted to it. Our feelings, our ideas aren't adapted to it. Human dimensions in general aren't adapted to it, because up to that point time was measured with our human dimensions. Perhaps this had already changed with the atomic bomb, and yet it was after Chernobyl that time took on a radically new dimension. Time transformed itself into eternity. The end and the beginning were joined. You went into the contaminated zone and met people who had stayed there, refusing to be evacuated: they cut the grass with a scythe, cultivated the earth with a plough, chopped down trees with an axe, spent their evenings by torchlight and, at the same time, the physicists were trying to solve puzzling problems, problems of unrivalled complexity posed by Chernobyl. Chernobyl is a totally new reality, completely beyond us, beyond our culture, beyond our biological potential.

P.V.: Let us stay with this theme of the historical accident. A historical accident characterizes a particular age. There is a kind of accident that happens in the prehistoric age or in the historical age. Can we say that Chernobyl is a post-historical accident, that is to say, one which overturns the longue durée of months and centuries, and hence of history, and takes us into a timescale that is post-historical, a timescale whose reference is to astronomy? If there is something that is not really historic in the human sense, it is surely astronomy—the time of the universe, the time, as I would put it, of creation. My feeling is that, with this tragedy we have come up against, not the end of history, as Fukuyama said, but a historical break that has no reference to what comes after. What is history? It is a time in which events succeed one another. That is to say, there is a before, a during and an after. Here, the after has no reference. The time preceding the accident is a time that does not communicate with the time that comes after it. The meltdown of the reactor melts down historical science. Why? Because accidents had always been local before. They had always been linked to a particular object—a flood or something of the sort. In this case, the accident is global. It embraces the whole future of the world: the future of the living species, animal and human. I'll take an example from this global accident: when the liquidators bury earth in the earth, this is an absolute absurdity. You don't bury earth in earth!

S.A.: You know, we grew up in a materialistic country. We fought religion, fought God. You might say that God was driven out of our lives. Suddenly it turned out that His presence was indispensable: all the churches were full, particularly on the first days after the accident. The people—communist and non-communist—began wearing little crosses they had previously been hiding away in drawers. The three-dimensional world of physics suddenly became too narrow. It couldn't give us any explanation. And people changed before my eyes, transformed themselves into different persons. They found themselves alone with their misfortune: the state deceived them and abandoned them to their loneliness. Philosophy, literature and the human sciences in general proved powerless. Admittedly, thinkers tried to give some kind of explanation in conventional terms, but you had only to go into the contaminated zone and experience fear at

touching an apple or sitting on the grass—the fear experienced even in looking at the gigantic flowers, greatly beyond normal size, that grew there—to realize that we were now living in a different, frightening world that defied explanation. People tried to hang on to anything: to physics, to religion. But if religion at least provided consolation, physics explained nothing at all. And people, left to their loneliness, set about pursuing knowledge by their own means. They opened their eyes. On the one hand, they were witnesses to a social catastrophe: an enormous Empire, which had deceived people and been incapable of helping them, was breaking up. And, on the other hand, the people who had lived in the materialistic world, as though imprisoned in a cage (for materialism is a revolt against the infinite), understood they had been pitched into that infinite. It was a very strong impression, this lone human being. I constantly had the impression, in speaking to these people, that I was observing not the past, but the future.

P.V.: In the end, there, materialistic philosophy fell into the trap of an accident, which was no longer that of substance, of matter, but a knowledge accident. The victim of the Chernobyl accident was science, knowledge. And even consciousness. If we take the accident that happens to substances, this means the collapse of a mountain, a flood, a plane crash etc. Now, in this case, the accident happened to science itself or, in other words, to knowledge. Something hit knowledge in its reality. And that something is effectively what we can call spirit, but we can also call it quite simply consciousness. The consciousness accident is also a reality. We had an extraordinary example of it with Auschwitz. Now, in a way, Chernobyl, like Auschwitz, and also like Hiroshima, is a consciousness accident. So we have three accidents in one or an accident triptych: the substance accident (the power station explodes), the knowledge accident (it is the very knowledge of the atomic physicists which in some sense is outstripped by the event) and, lastly, there is the accident befalling consciousness itself—that is to say, there is no insight into this event; it exceeds consciousness. We have three accidents in one, like the Russian dolls, the matrioshkas.

S.A.: You know, it was a very strange sensation. You come into this zone in a very ordinary 4x4 and you immediately plunge into an environment of evil, of death. And you are incapable of recognizing this evil and death, because they are present in a new guise. And consciousness comes to a stop. You are totally right. Consciousness, confronted with this, found itself confused and in disarray. People tried either to act by inertia—the inertia of culture, the inertia of the state—or to close their eyes. It was the reaction of the simple folk that was the most interesting. They were more open because they were not in the grip of culture; so they entered this new world and tried to understand it, to get a handle on it in some way. It was very interesting to observe how, when consciousness refused to function, the subconscious took over. At first the story went around that they were taking bodies away in their thousands to bury them in secret places, because the urge was to see immediate victims. Victims fit with our conception of time. Either the bullet kills you now or you die in hospital quickly. Now, in this case death stretched over several generations. It was a new death, the mechanics of which had just been set in train. And this particular mechanism was set to run for centuries. It was at that point that the subconscious began to dig up ancestral fears: people spoke of monsters, of many-headed children, of headless fish swimming in the rivers, of birds with extraordinary life spans but no offspring. It was the children who asked the most extraordinary questions. To me, that was splendid: they asked basic philosophical questions, they had all the makings of philosophers. The children asked, for example, if the fish and the birds were going to have their young. The old people tried to remember something similar from their past experience, as though they had already experienced this. It was very interesting to observe how human beings sought new props in this new world, whereas official propaganda and culture and philosophy were paralysed and silent. It seems to me that if we had understood Chernobyl, we would have written more about it. We are paralysed by the knowledge of our ignorance.

P.V.: I am a child of the war, of the Second World War. The other aspect that struck me about Chernobyl was the confusion between war and accident. In the testimonies you heard: It isn't war and yet it's war. Why all these soldiers, these armoured cars, these helicopters in the sky? We aren't at war, there isn't an enemy. Who is the enemy? How do we fight? The reference to warfare became the major reference and there was no let up in that. The only comparable example was world war: "Great War," to employ the expression they used in 1914-18. It seems to me there is something absolutely new in this. I mean, the global accident we have spoken of is also an accident that relates to the nature of relations between human beings. With human beings, we're either at peace or at war, with declarations of war, clashes, battles. Here, suddenly, what replaces war is an accident on such a scale that it requires the defence forces of a nation to deal with it, requires a new vigilance etc. As though the Chernobyl accident foreshadowed a new kind of warfare, terrorist war—wars in which you cannot differentiate between attacks and accidents, where the declaration of war does not exist, where there are no uniforms, no flags, where there is simply evil-doing. The wilful evil-doing of a terrorist or the involuntary, spontaneous evil-doing of an accident, as I would put it. I think what we are experiencing in the world at the moment is an indeterminacy between war and accidents. Accidents have attained such levels of damage, of mortality, of long-lastingness that they have outrun traditional warfare, that is to say that the rule-governed clash between human beings, with a political dimension (Clausewitz: war is the continuation of politics by other means) has suddenly been replaced by the major accident, such as that at Chernobyl. In my opinion, there is here a very great danger that, in the future, terror attacks and accidents will be used to destabilize an enemy. This is a thing that worries me greatly today.

S.A.: One of the very strong impressions of the first years, if not in fact the first months, after the catastrophe is when you begin to understand that the image of the enemy has totally changed. Our old miltary culture, our old military literature doesn't work here any more. And I remember how the father of Khodymchuk wept, the power-station operative who had pressed the button and, as a result, triggered the accident. The whole chain of events which led to the explosion was concentrated in that operative. The blown-up reactor and the sarcophagus are in fact a memorial to that man since he was blown to pieces inside it. But they made a tomb for him at the cemetery. And the old man would go to the graveside, always alone. People walked by and snarled at him: "It's your son who blew us up." Because they needed to see an enemy. And in this case, it was a simple operative. I remember his father saying, "What makes you say that? He was so kind. He adored kittens. He used to take lost frogs back to the pond. He was a good boy." It suddenly turned out that a normal, ordinary man can kill us, a man who simply goes to his work, a man with no terroristic ideas in mind. A man who will quite simply be a link in a chain of technical circumstances. And this new image of the enemy was so incomprehensible. Similarly, when people were evacuated, the old people got down on their knees by their houses and said, "Where is the war?" At the time we weren't ready for the question. Today you know the answer. But we couldn't tell them: yes, it's war, but a new kind of war and new times. In Sweden, I often hear people say we are going to outlaw nuclear power stations here and we shall be safe. But that safe world doesn't exist any longer today. You can sit in the café sipping a drink and something will blow elsewhere, at the other end of the world, and we shall then die slowly, without knowing we are dying. We have entered a period of evil which doesn't make any announcements, doesn't show itself and knows no laws: we have entered a darkened world.

P.V.: As regards that situation, in France we had the contaminated blood affair. On that occasion a woman minister said: "As minister and secretary of state for health, I accept I am responsible, but not guilty." The phrase, "responsible, but not guilty" is a very important one. And I wonder if it isn't the same question that arises where the authorities responsible for running the Chernobyl power plant are concerned. Are they responsible, but not guilty? If they are neither responsible, nor guilty, what are they? This is one of the great questions. Why? Because guilt and responsibility are elements of justice. It is a commonplace point. Now, given the scale of the tragedy, both of the contaminated blood in France and the Chernobyl catastrophe, we get beyond the question of guilt. First, to apportion only responsibility—I am thinking here of the contaminated blood, with the minister who says, "I feel responsible, but not guilty". But, when it comes to Chernobyl, can we say there is someone responsible for the power station blowing up? In my view, we have passed beyond responsibility. At a first stage, we passed beyond guilt, with the very serious accident of the contaminated blood. At a second stage, by way of all you've said about philosophy and the crisis of consciousness, it's the responsibility of the actors themselves that can be contested. If there's someone or something responsible today, who or what is it? It's techno-science itself. That is to say, not some particular scientist, not some official from a particular power station or whatever. But a science with no awareness of its risks, of its dangers, of its potential tragedies is a science responsible for its perversities, of which Chernobyl is a major example. The involvement of physicists in nuclear science posed questions about the responsibility of science with the Oppenheimer affair among others. The Chernobyl affair raises the same question where civil nuclear power is concerned, rather than its military use. The same question of responsibility—not just of one individual or another, but of science itself. To pose such questions is not to put science on trial, but to develop a new understanding of an accident which passes beyond traditional guilt and traditional civil responsibility. And this raises a major question for the lawyers and, hence, for reason. And for justice.

S.A.: I think it may be a question here not just of science, but of the whole image of the world we have built up in our heads. It is a question of our hierarchy of values, our value-system. After Chernobyl, the entire construction of our world seems to have cracked. And the intellectuals or the physicists or the philosophers are not the only ones to understand this. The most interesting thing is what goes on at the level of the consciousness of the masses. The people do not insult and persecute the scientists who come into the contaminated zone to measure levels of radiation in the soil and the like. To take another example, the manager of the power station was judged by the old scale of values: as manager, he was held responsible for the accident and convicted of it. We are not yet advanced enough in my country to judge science. And when he ended up in prison, his family were afraid the other inmates would kill him. They were afraid the prisoners would really see him as guilty and lynch him. But it turned out in reality that these simple folk had understood the whole thing. They had understood he was just the last link in the chain, and that the guilt had imperatively to be pinned on someone. And it was pinned on him. That is to say that, after Chernobyl, we didn't think things through: we didn't think through how we had approached a frontier of horror no longer commensurable with our human time, with our moral laws—for none of these things operate any longer in this new space. And here the question of collective and individual responsibility is posed in new terms. It emerged that, in catastrophes of this kind, it hardly matters what sort of person one is: honest or dishonest, good or bad, a professional or an incompetent specialist. The over-arching character of this catastrophe shows itself in the total destruction of the human world organized by the old laws.

P.V.: We cannot end our conversation without a word about the liquidators. They were extremely important characters, not just for Byelorussia and the USSR, but also for Europe. We are dealing here with individuals who are the opposite of those who commit suicide in order to kill. They died to save lives, they died in the hundreds in horrendous conditions. In them, we saw the development of a heroism that is not at all like that of the soldiers of Stalingrad or elsewhere. This is the beginning of something entirely new. They were prophets.

Text translated from French by Chris Turner

Svetlana Aleksievich and Paul Virilio during the filming of *Unknown Quantity* by **Andrei Ujica** Photo taken by Dorcas Müller in the Large Studio HfG Karlsruhe on September 28, 2002

Inspired by Evil
(excerpts from the Chernobyl diary[1])

Svetlana Aleksievich

For ten years, I wrote a book on Chernobyl, the most incredible event of the twentieth century. From this time forth, we forever abandoned the idea of a future without evil, of a better future; we began to live in a world where traces of an Evil inspiration can be found everywhere, where Evil wears new masks, where Manhattan goes next to Chernobyl…

Throughout all those years, I kept a journal, of which some passages were incorporated in my book *Voices from Chernobyl*[2] and others never published. This journal constitutes an important account of the personal experiences and feelings that people underwent during the first days and the first months after the catastrophe—an account of the encounter between mankind before Chernobyl and mankind of Chernobyl…

The nuclear reactor burns… Our newspapers had long kept their silence, and now they lie without scruple. They immediately launched into the "canticle" of Chernobyl, an exact copy of the news broadcasted during the Second World War (despite the passage of half a century). Once again we read the proud titles: "The Atom Has Been Conquered," "The Exploit of Chernobyl," "How to Create Soviet Character," etc. At the same time, we listen on the sly to programs in Russian on the American radio station "Liberty," we whisper news into each other's ears. We scour pharmacies in search of iodine—upon the recommendation of the aforementioned radio station, not of our doctors. The latter advise us not to give in to panic and not to believe "enemy radio stations." Meanwhile, everyone knows that many doctors take protective measures themselves and tell their close friends and family to do the same. What ever happened to the Hippocratic oath? A friend commented: "Here, there are no doctors, teachers, scientists, or journalists; there is only one profession: the Soviet man…"

We have been thrust into the cosmos, into a new reality. But we are still the same.

Yesterday, my father called (he taught history for forty years in a rural school): "This is certainly the diversionary tactics of Western secret services. The KGB is already carrying out an investigation at the power plant. The spies and saboteurs will be found. The Soviet court will judge them."

My dear Papa… We can talk to him about the new orchard he just planted last spring, but not the government, about angling and Peter the Great, but not communism, about life and death in general, but not what is happening to us.

My parents live in a village a hundred kilometers from Chernobyl[3]…

This week I overheard a neighbor, a female engineer, telling the people in our building: "At the freight station, entire wagons are loaded with the burnt cadavers of men and animals. These are astonishing cadavers, not black but pink. They are taken to Siberia and buried there."

By what strange route has the past come back to us: under Stalin, wagons of prisoners were taken to Siberia to fill the gulags…

It was a five-year-old boy who asked me the most gripping question during one of my trips in the contaminated zone: "Ma'am, you write and you have read lots of books, so tell me: will the fish have their babies? Will the birds have their chicks? And our pregnant cow Rose, will she be able to give birth to her calf?"

Taken by surprise, we have been thrust into a new reality… How can we explain something we cannot even imagine?

Still recently, official propaganda proclaimed: "The beneficial effects of the pacific Soviet atom—for every family!" Today this slogan is a terrible reality. The academician Alexandrov, the godfather of our nuclear power plants, often repeated (and we believed him!) that the nuclear power plants were so safe they could be built in the middle of Moscow, in Red Square. These power plants, he would say, were as harmless as samovars and as easy to handle.

We dreaded a nuclear war, a nuclear bomb. Nobody had yet imagined that the military atom and the pacific atom were allies, partners. One thing is clear today: the face of the enemy has changed. And despite all our attempts to go into hiding, even from ourselves, nothing will protect us. No technology will act as a shield for us. The catastrophes are no longer accidents; they are the principal product of our civilization.

Books and films have often portrayed the Apocalypse, but reality has proven to be even more fantastic.

During my first journey to the contaminated zone, I suddenly realized that I was scared of everything that was good and harmless in the past. I was scared to eat an apple, scared to lean against a tree, scared to sit on the grass. Everything was the same as before—forms, colors, smells, names—but it was a different world. Another space. A world where everything could kill me: soil, water, berries… rain… wind… I found myself confronted with new faces of evil. Death was on the prowl, decked out in appearances I did not recognize. It concealed itself. And all our past experiences of fear became useless.

All of our instruments of defense were failing us: this evil could not be touched, seen, heard, smelled, or tasted—our eyes, ears, nose, and fingers could do nothing about it. Death had infiltrated everything. It ruled.

Reality slips away, fades… How can we understand where we have ended up… what is happening here… now… to us… to me…

We could define what we are now experiencing in one word: fear. Fear is someone that lives inside of us, a separate being, an unknown. Fear is the eventuality of finding oneself outside of the limits of our lives, of traditional physics, of culture. In the course of my encounters and conversations with very different people, I hear the same old refrain: "I never read anything like this," "nobody ever told me about anything like this," "I never saw anything like this in the movies." Party officials, from the biggest to the smallest, generals and colonels, soldiers, scientists, doctors—all are disconcerted.

I prefer talking with children or old farmers—spontaneous poets and philosophers whose inner worlds best withstand the ordeal. For the rest of us, we can only recognize that we do not measure up to what has happened to us. The past, which seemed to be a reliable resource (like a world archive), has suddenly become powerless. Many people are seeking consolation in prayer… The churches are full…

I read in a newspaper that four days after the catastrophe, Chernobyl's clouds were already hovering over Africa and China. The Earth has suddenly become so small…

I hear completely new utterances everywhere. In the bus, in the subway, on the landing outside my door. We get used to the new reality… I start understanding that I am tracking it like a detective. I listen, I hasten to write everything down, my ear is constantly open; sometimes I feel like I have metamorphosed into one huge ear.

There is no doubt about the importance of what is happening.

Two catastrophes occurred at the same time: a cosmic catastrophe, that of Chernobyl, and the other, a historic one, the burial of the gigantic socialist continent. The latter is simpler to understand; it is more within the reach of ordinary people. We endlessly discuss inflation and its price increases, we talk about Lenin (was he a criminal or a Russian idealist?) and Marx (was he right or wrong?). Chernobyl, to the contrary, is a new challenge since, for the first time, humanity is confronted with the cosmos.

The details of the accident do not matter so much for me: exactly what happened that night at the power plant, who is responsible, what decisions were taken, how many tons of sand and concrete must we pour to construct a sarcophagus over the devil's lair? Instead, I probe the utterances of people hit by the unknown, by a mystery that remains to be solved. I want to establish the history of our sentiments. How do they evolve? What could human beings learn about themselves? How have they adapted to new bounds of horror? Has their world changed? And their representation of their place in this world? In this divine world.

Before Chernobyl, I journeyed in the suffering of others: the Second World War, Afghanistan, the suicides related to the collapse of the Soviet empire. With Chernobyl, I myself am simultaneously a participant and a witness. My life is part of the event since I live in the very land of Chernobyl. In little Belarus, which the world had never heard of in the past.

Henceforth, we are known, for we no longer live so much in an ordinary country as in the laboratory of Chernobyl. Chernobyl has entered our lives for hundreds and thousands of years (such is the life span of certain radioactive elements) and it will accompany us eternally. "We are Chernobylians," say the Belarusians as if they formed a new nation, a new people. Chernobyl has become our home, our national destiny. Will it not supplant our history to remain in the collective memory of humanity as its unique event? An incommensurable event, which stretches beyond our world, which surpasses a human life span. We cannot embrace it, we can only follow it.

Chernobyl is more than a catastrophe… And the attempt to put it on the list of supposedly similar catastrophes prevents us from thinking about what happened. The more I travel in the contaminated zones, the more I talk to people and the more I have the impression of jotting down in my notebook not the present or the past, but the future.

Yesterday, for example, I met Lioucia Ignatenk, the wife of a fireman. Her husband participated in the extinction of the fire on the reactor's rooftop and within the power plant building the first night after the explosion. A night squad of firemen, they were barely more than ten and, by the early hours of the morning, each had received a dose of radiation surpassing the norm a thousand times over. They were transported to Moscow in a military aircraft, then treated in a specialized clinic. Lioucia was pregnant. She hurried to Moscow but all information on the irradiated victims was classified as confidential, as it is the custom in our country. Of course, it was just an open secret. The first militiaman she asked told her how to get to the aforementioned clinic. And this is what the doctors told her. Lines worthy of Shakespeare: "You will enter the room and you will see your husband. He will look the same as usual or almost but he is a different person. He has the same eyes, the same ears, the same hair, but you cannot draw near him. You cannot caress him. You cannot kiss him. You can only look at him. He is no longer a human being but a radioactive object that must be deactivated. He has 'radiation sickness'... He has two weeks to live..."

I listened to her and I promptly understood what kind of book I had to write. A book for humanity that will reveal the new "experiences" brought by this event. Like the "black box" of an airplane, Belarusians had recorded information for the future. Information on the fears of the future...

Notes from the first days

Nadejda Vygovskaïa, evacuee from the city of Pripyat: "It happened during the night of Friday to Saturday... In the morning, no one suspected anything. There was just an unpleasant smoky odor in the air. I sent my son off to school and my husband went to the barber's. I was preparing lunch when my husband suddenly returned: 'A fire started at the power plant. We are advised to stay tuned to the radio.' At the time, we lived in Pripyat, not very far away from the reactor. During the night, we witnessed an extraordinary spectacle... Still today, I have that reactor, which appeared illuminated from within, before my very eyes. The entire sky was glowing. It was not an ordinary fire, but a very dense raspberry-pink glow. I never saw anything like it in the movies. I never read a description of the like. In the evening, people went out on their balconies and those who did not have one went to the homes of friends and family. We were living on the ninth floor and had a panoramic view. People brought their children out onto the balconies, lifted them up in their arms and said: 'Look at how beautiful it is! Remember this image!' They were engineers, technicians, and operators who worked at the power plant. There were also physics professors. We stayed in the black dust... We talked... We breathed... We admired... Some came from afar, driving their cars or riding their bikes ten kilometers to see it. We did not know that death could be so beautiful..."

Ivan Jmykhov, chemical engineer: "Six months after the accident, I was recruited... Within two days, we were given military uniforms and we were sent to the zone. We called it the 'apocalypse zone' and people passed around a copy of the Bible there. Everyone wanted to read it, in search of prophecies that could be compared with what we were going through. We were doing a simple but strange job there, which no one has ever done before: we washed houses, streets, trees, bushes... We buried earth in earth: we removed the upper layer of the contaminated ground, loaded it in dumpsters and transported it in special coffins. We lifted the ground and rolled it up like a carpet in huge rolls. Picture a green lawn with grass, flowers, roots... with beetles... butterflies... spiders... earthworms... Green, red, oranges... There were thousands of them. Millions. I had never thought, never understood that there could be so many living beings in the soil. I did not know their names. No name at all. That is what we were doing: we buried earth in earth... A ludicrous task... After we were through, it looked like a moonscape: extremely white sand, yellow earth, depopulated... A strange beauty. Like on the Moon. With no trace of human life, time itself flows differently.

We arrived in a village, a large village of about three hundred houses but, since the explosion, they have all been empty, all evacuated. The only one left was an old woman. She was hiding. We entered her house nevertheless. 'My sons, don't touch me! she cried, clutching an icon. I will not leave my land. Is there a war? I lived through the war: they fire, they bomb, everything burns, and foreign soldiers occupy the villages. But here, in my home, the orchard is in bloom, the birds are singing, onions are sprouting in my garden, a small mouse lives there, together with some sparrows. Is that what you call war?'"

At the time, none of us knew it was war. A different kind of war...

Anastasia Ivanovna Koultchitskaïa, retiree: "I will tell you two things. One day, when some soldiers were at our home, which is nearby the woods, a moose entered the yard. Animals would often come: wild bores, hares, foxes. They are not afraid since almost everyone left the village. A soldier spotted the moose and immediately aimed his rifle at it. My husband and I held him back, begging: 'Stop, don't do it! God forbid, don't shoot. The animals are like family to us. We live the same misfortune.' And the militia told us to wash the logs, not to eat the eggs from our chickens, not to drink

210

milk from our cow, not to cook our potatoes. Who could have imagined that even something baked in the oven would be inedible. The timeless order of our lives is gone. We cannot even drink our water."

What am I looking for? I am looking for a shattered man… One who felt alone in the face of eternity, who utters new lines…

I answer the phone, the voice of a stranger says to me: "I heard you are gathering information for a book on Chernobyl. We must meet each other. But hurry." Speaking to him on the phone, I find out that this man was a helicopter pilot. He unloaded bags of sand above the burning reactor. Now, he was seriously ill. We met each other a few days later. When a tall six-and-a-half-foot shadow opened the door and said to me "I am an Ego covered with skin," I understood why he asked me to hurry. "Fortunately you arrived in time, doctors give me one or two months to live. I wanted to tell someone… To leave my story behind… We have not understood everything, but have seen much. It must be written down. It must be remembered. I did not understand what had happened to us, perhaps you do not understand either, but others will understand… later… after we are gone…"

Letter from a mother who had just lost her three-year-old daughter: "I am no longer afraid of death. My daughter lay so beautifully in her coffin, like a doll. And no one noticed that she was missing two fingers on her right hand. I was in tears—how would she be in heaven? She is missing two fingers all the same, and she is a girl."

Encounter with refugees from Tajikistan and Armenia in the market town of Narovlya. Over there, there is war and bloodshed. They have nowhere to go. Nobody is waiting for them anywhere. Great Russia hardly concerns itself with little people… Currently, twenty-five million Russians live outside of its borders in former Soviet republics. Another Russia. In the contaminated regions of Belarus, abandoned houses, entire streets of villages and small towns, are being repopulated. Two human streams cross over: while people born and bred Belarusians are fleeing the zone, refugees coming from the confines of the ex-Soviet empire are arriving.

A family wishing to remain anonymous for fear of reprisals: "We are less frightened here in Belarus than over there," says the daughter. "I am scared of the men with rifles. That is the most horrible thing. We have lived through atrocities… Just imagine… People who work together, who invite each other to their homes and gather round the same table. Then some came to

the houses of others with machine guns, screaming: 'Russians, get out of here! Go home to Russia! Out!' We found ourselves without a homeland. Our Homeland was the Soviet Union but it does not exist anymore. And that time exists no more. Nor do the people. We are not Russians, we are Soviets. It is our nationality. My mother is Russian and my father is Ukrainian. Who am I?… There is plenty of land in Belarus. People have abandoned it, nobody wants it. We will not be driven away from here…" The mother: "From now on, our home is here. Chernobyl is our home. People ask us if we are scared. But we do not know the kind of fear they are talking about, it is not inscribed in our memory. I know what the plague, cholera, and war are. But who knows what Chernobyl is. Here, it is like anywhere. The grass grows, birds sing. There is a statue of Lenin. And nobody is shooting."

Throughout history, war has always served as the measuring rod of horror. But Chernobyl has changed everything, including our relationship to fear, time, and geography. It seems to me that we have lost immortality, that we have lost eternity.

I went to the inauguration of the first monument to the victims of Chernobyl. It reminded me of our war monuments. We are already living in the future, within the future, whereas our culture, our thoughts, and our feelings are in the past.

When consciousness recedes, so does culture… It is the subconscious that functions… I wrote down some rumors that circulated persistently:

"The dead are picked up in villages nearby the power plant, they are transported to cemeteries in buses and dumpsters, and buried by the thousands in communal graves. Just like during the Leningrad blockade…"

"Pikes with no heads and no fins have been caught in the rivers and lakes. They are just floating bellies…"

"The animals in the forest are suffering from 'radiation sickness.' They are in a pitiful state. Hunters are scared of them and feel sorry for them. They cannot bring themselves to shoot them."

Increasingly, history is presenting itself to me as a history of human fears, as the life of our fears…

An old beekeeper: "On that day… I went to the orchard in the morning. It was already white with blossoms. But I felt as if something were missing, a habitual sound, then I understood: I did not hear the buzzing of the bees anymore. The beehives, dozens of them, were under the apple trees. What was happening? I put on my mask to check: the bees were in the hives, silent. They would not come out and were not buzzing. They still refused to come out of their hives the day after, and the day after that… I thought they had fallen ill… they were poisoned by the inorganic fertilizer of the kolkhoz fields, by something chemical… Much later, two weeks after, we were informed of an accident at the power plant, just thirty kilometers from our village. We were aware of nothing. The bees, they knew straight away."

A milkmaid: "On that day… In the evening, the shepherds returned with the herd; they were surprised and puzzled… At noon, when they arrived at the river, the cows had refused to drink. The shepherds pressed them but they drew back immediately… Nobody understood. Several days later, the explosion at Chernobyl was announced on the radio. The Pripyat's water was contaminated…"

A boy: "On that day… I woke up in the morning. I whistled to call a friend. We took our bikes and went fishing. We stopped at the entrance of the village to dig up some worms. We knew of a spot nearby an old stable where there were lots of them. We dug and dug, but did not find a single little earthworm. They had all burrowed deep into the earth. Maybe a meter deep. No one believed us at home… Several days went by. Everybody started talking about Chernobyl. But my story about the earthworms was from the very day of the accident… It was an enigma… When I asked my biology teacher about it, even he could not provide an explanation…"

I scan the world with new eyes…

Whose place on the Earth is more secure, more eternal? Human beings or them: birds, bees, June bugs, plants? We should learn from their techniques for survival. We should learn what they know, what they retain in their memory, in their culture, in their civilization.

Here in the zone, the distance between them and I is shrinking. There is no longer that gulf that separated us in the past.

Everything is life. All of us, we are living time.

When the scientists from the Belarus Academy of Science discussed the evacuation of contaminated regions, one question arose: what should we do with the animals? Human beings always think about themselves and write about themselves. But many other beings live in our midst. What should we do with them? How can they be protected? Herds of cows and horses can be moved away from the contaminated zones… Geese, chickens, and ducks can be transported. But what about the animals living in the forest and in swamps? What about the birds in the sky or the insects in the earth?

In the end, people abandoned the zone and left the animals there. Later, the animals were shot… Thus arises the question of our responsibility to the natural world. What right do we have to condemn the animals?

Sometimes, it seems to me that we like to be afraid. Effectively, we are obsessed by a death that becomes our only future. But it is no longer an old woman holding a scythe; it is a beautiful woman… a great beauty…

We are all united by fear—the strong and the weak, the rich and the poor, the happy and the unhappy. And it is henceforth clear that we have nowhere to hide… no army or police force can defend us. No distance, no comfort, no missile, no aircraft, no destroyer can protect us. Nothing and no one will come to our rescue! What do "near" and "far" signify? What is the meaning of "our people" and "the others"? After Chernobyl, our culture has become nothing but a trunk full of old manuscripts…

I met a Japanese scientist in the zone and I asked him what he was doing there: "Preparing ourselves for the future," he replied.

I thought about the artistic character of Evil, about Evil as form of knowledge. Life often challenges us to believe in its veracity. I suddenly felt to what extent my faith in documents was naive. The document, after all, is just a human version of reality. It is an infatuation. Humans have wholly invested themselves in it: they put their knowledge and ignorance, their beliefs, superstitions, in short, their entire life in it. Our human lives, so small and imperfect.

Art is a struggle against the disappearance of traces and the idea that we will disappear, that we will go through life without leaving behind a trace, cannot even be fathomed. On the one hand, there is nothing authentic about our stay on Earth since reality continually eludes any attempt to grasp it and, on the other hand, we constantly yearn for happiness. In a sense, we yearn for a sign. The world in three dimensions agrees less and less with the modern human being. We find it too cramped. Mankind tries to break through to some far away place… into inconceivable, inaccessible infinity…

How did Chernobyl change me? With tenacious and rapacious claws, it definitively snatched me away from materialism. At the end of the day, materialism is a revolt against infinity, against mystery.

212

On the street: "Now I am scared of everything. I am scared to buy cottage cheese or berries or anything else at the farmers' market. And even when I buy cottage cheese in a store, I wonder from what milk it was made, where it could have come from."

"They arrived at a neighbor's house and he was taken as a reservist to participate in the decontamination work. People are afraid. When they are drafted, they do not show up at the recruitment bureau. So the army comes to get them at home. They lie in wait for them."

"This is how they came for my husband, in the middle of the night, to bring him to the zone. There was a knock at the door: 'You have fifteen minutes to pack your bags!' I am happy I have two children, a boy and a girl. For no one knows what may happen when my husband returns… It is said that over there…"

"I cannot read the newspapers anymore. The words they employ are from wartime: evacuation, atom, explosion… The war is ever present in my mind. I was a little girl at the time, but I remember everything as if it were yesterday."

"Before, the most horrible thing was war. And now, it is Chernobyl. But what is radiation? Who has seen it? What does it look like: white, gray?"

"My mother called: the village is now being evacuated. A bus was sent to take the children first but the president of the kolkhoz had the bus loaded with his furniture, rugs, sacks of potatoes, and canned food. Even if it were the end of the world, people would remain the same—faithless, sinners…"

"Before, we gathered dead leaves in the parks and burned them; now, we bury them…"

"My husband is a taxi driver. He comes home from work and takes valium. His heart is failing him. He says that, every day, three or four birds in flight will collide into his car. They are perishing, of course. They no longer have the strength to fly high. They huddle up on balconies as if they had gone crazy."

In a maternity ward: "As soon as I give birth, show me the baby. I want to check his hands and feet. My husband worked on the construction of Chernobyl's sarcophagus…"

"Yesterday, a woman gave birth to a girl. Two fingers are missing on each hand. And she is such a pretty young woman."

"How can we make love? My husband and I are scared… We come from Chernobyl…"

"I dream of having a boy. A strong and handsome boy. I love my husband so much! I am happy. But we have not been able to have children. We left Chernobyl two years ago. Only that has changed nothing. Chernobyl is a weight we drag behind us."

In a theater: "The party demands that we put on a play about Chernobyl. Something heroic. An epic for the common man."

"We must avoid fiction and try to understand what is happening. We need a document. When reality is more incredible than any fiction, a document is called for."

"I would never direct a play on Chernobyl, just as I have never staged a show on war. Evil is much too seductive."

"A play was brought to us. A collection of horrors… We read it and we gave it back to the author… I am looking for something else: we must extract a meaning from this horror, try to describe the indescribable. If we succeed, the only thing left to do will be to forget."

What is my account about? The mysterious world of Evil. And the mystery of humanity.

The speech of human beings is capable of surpassing artistic form. Art does not suffice to make the profound testimony of mankind heard… There are scripts everywhere… Scripts… Each has his or her script. His or her secret. We only have to listen…

Notes

1. The accident at the Chernobyl nuclear power plant occurred on April 26, 1986.

2. Svetlana Aleksievich, *Voices from Chernobyl. Chronicle of the Future,* trans. Antonina W. Bouis (London: Aurum Press, 1999). Originally published as *Chernobylskaia molitva: khronika budushchego*/Svetlana Aleksievich (Moscow: Ostozhe, 1997).

3. Two years after Chernobyl, my thirty-five-year-old sister, a doctor by profession, died of cancer. My mother became totally blind. My father had renal cancer. And ten years later, in Ossovetz, the village where my parents lived in the province of Gomel, entire streets remained without inhabitants— they were all dead.

Translated from the French by Jian-Xing Too

Biographies

Svetlana Aleksievich

Born in Ukraine in 1948. Lives and works in Europe.

After studying journalism, Svetlana Aleksievich began her career as a journalist, publishing two books on World War II that provoked a controversy in her country. Her book on the war in Afghanistan, *Zinky Boys: Soviet Voices from the Afghanistan War* was subject to attacks from the communist and military press, who would not forgive her for unveiling the myth of the glorious Soviet army. Her last book entitled, *Voices from Chernobyl: Chronicle of the Future* is a stirring account of life after Chernobyl written from the hundreds of interviews she made with the witnesses and victims of the tragedy. Since October 2002, Svetlana Aleksievich has lived in France where she will spend two years, thanks to a grant from the Parlement des écrivains, an endowment which was in part instigated by urbanist-philosopher Paul Virilio and sociologist Pierre Bourdieu.

Selected Bibliography

Voices from Chernobyl: Chronicles of the Future,
Aurum Press, London, 1999

Zinky Boys: Soviet Voices from the Afghanistan War,
W.W. Norton and Company Editions, New York, 1992

Dominic Angerame

Born in 1949 in New York.
Lives, teaches and works in San Francisco.

Since 1969, Dominic Angerame has made more than 25 films that have been shown and have won awards in film festivals around the world. He has also been honored with two "Cine Probe" Series at the Museum of Modern Art in New York City—in 1993 and in 1998. Angerame teaches filmmaking/ cinema studies/criticism at the University of California, Berkeley Extension and the San Francisco Art Institute. He has also been a guest lecturer and visiting artist for Stanford University, the School of the Art Institute of Chicago, and others. Dominic Angerame has been the Executive Director of *Canyon Cinema* for the past twenty years, turning it into one of the world's most renowned distributors of avant-garde and experimental films. For the San Francisco Museum of Modern Art, he curated "Shake the nation", a series of fourteen films tracing the development of avant-garde filmmaking in San Francisco from 1939 to 1999. His work is very much influenced by the avant-garde filmmakers of the 1920's and 1930's and deals with the human cycle of destruction and construction that places the city environment in a constant state of change.

Recent Filmography

1997
City Symphony, (*Continuum, Deconstruction Sight, Premonition, In The Course of Human Events, Line of Fire*)
Line of Fire, 9 min
In The Course of Human Events, 23.5 min

1995
Premonition, 9 min

1990
Deconstruction Sight, 14 min

1987
Continuum, 17 min

Recent Screenings

San Francisco Art Institute, San Francisco, November 2000

Bilbao International Film Festival, Guggenheim Museum, Bilbao, November 2000

Anthology Film Archives, New York, October 2000

Machida City Museum of Graphic Arts, Tokyo, July 2000

Caligari-Film Bühne, Wiesbaden, June 2000

Recent articles

"The City As Motion Picture: Notes on Some California City Films," Scott MacDonald, *Wide Angel Magazine, City Scapes I*, Vol. 19 #4, October 1997

"Epilogue," Wheeler Dixon, *The Exploding Eye: A Re-Visionary History of American Experimental Film*, 1997

"Review of *In the Course of Human Events* by Dominic Angerame," Silke Tudor, *San Francisco Weekly*, 28 May – 3 June 1997

"Imaginary Light – the film Premonition by Dominic Angerame," uncredited, *Oxygen: A Spirited Literary Magazine*, N° 14, 1995

Jem Cohen

Born in 1962. Lives and works in New York.

Jem Cohen is a New York based filmmaker. His work over the past 18 years has been built from his own ongoing archive of street footage, portraits, and sound. Cohen mixes documentary, narrative, and experimental genres, as well as film and video.
The projects he creates from his archives defy easy categorisation. His works range from personal and political city portraits made on his travels around the world to poetic documents of daily life and its ephemeral moments. His works have been broadcast by the BBC, PBS, The Sundance Channel, Planete, and TVE-Europe and are in the collections of the Museum of Modern Art of New York and of the Whitney Museum in New York. Jem Cohen has been the recipient of fellowships from the Guggenheim and Rockefeller Foundations.

Recent filmography

2002
Chain, installation

2000
Benjamin Smoke, 80 min
Little Flags, 6 min

1999
Instrument, 1 hour 55 min
Blood Orange Sky, 25 min
Amber City, 48 min

1998
Lucky Three, 11 min

1996
Lost Book Found, 37 min

Recent Exhibitions/Screenings

2001
Retrospectives: National Film Theatre, London; Oberhausen Film Festival, Oberhausen

Benjamin Smoke, Berlin International Film Festival; Edinburgh International Film Festival; Melbourne International Film Festival; London International Film Festival; Wexner Center for the Arts, Ohio; Walker Art Center, Minneapolis

Little Flags, Melbourne International Film Festival; Cinema Texas Short Film Festival

1999
Instrument, Whitney Biennial; broadcast, The Sundance Channel; International Film Festival Rotterdam; Boston Museum of Fine Arts; The Lux Center, London

Recent Articles

"Punk Poet," Kieron Corless, *Time Out London*, February 2001

"Do You Recognize this Scene?" SF Said, *The Daily Telegraph*, February 2001

"Beating a Path to the Movies" SF Said, *The Daily Telegraph*, January 2001

"A Captivating Wit, Drawing His Way Toward Death," Luc Sante, *New York Times*, July 2000

"Jem Cohen, Fugazi, Instrument," David Wilson, *PunkPlanet*, September/October 1999

Bruce Conner

Born in 1933 in McPherson, Kansas.
Lives and works in San Francisco.

After receiving his B.F.A in art in 1956, Bruce Conner moved to San Francisco where he became a key figure in the burgeoning Beat community. He first attracted public attention with moody nylons-shrouded assemblages, which were complex amalgams of found objects often combined with collaged or painted surfaces.

During the late 1950s, Conner began making short movies in a singular style that has established him as one of the most important figures in post-war independent filmmaking. His innovative technique can be best seen in his first film, *A MOVIE* (1958), an editing *tour de force* made entirely by piecing together scraps of B-movie condensations, newsreels, novelty shorts, and other pre-existing footage. In *A MOVIE*, Conner critically focuses on American pop culture, examining its deeper forms of ideological meaning and the ethical consequences of a society enthralled with speed, conquest and power. In recent years Conner has continued to work on a small scale, producing collages and inkblot drawings.

Recent Filmography

1959-1967/1996

LOOKING FOR MUSHROOMS, 14,5 min

1963-1964/1995

TELEVISION ASSASSINATION, 14 min

1981

AMERICA IS WAITING, 3,5 min

MEA CULPA, 5 min

1978

MONGOLOID, 3,5 min

Recent Exhibitions

2002

Bruce Conner, Collages 1966-1996, Alan Koppel Gallery, Chicago

Bruce Conner, Intaglio Prints, Illustrations for "The ballad of Lemon and Crow" by Glenn Todd, Arion Press Gallery, Presidio, San Francisco

2002 B.C., presentation of 8 films by Bruce Conner on DVD, Michael Kohn Gallery, Los Angeles and Paule Anglim Gallery, San Francisco

2001

Bruce Conner, Susan Inglett, New York

2000

2000 BC: The Bruce Conner Story Part II, Museum of Contemporary Art, Los Angeles

Bruce Conner, Early Assemblages and Recent Inkblots, Kohn Turner Gallery, Los Angeles

Dead Punks and Ashes, Curt Marcus Gallery, New York

1999

Looking for Mushrooms. Bruce Conner Drawings 1960 to 1968, Kohn Turner Gallery, Los Angeles

Cai Guo-Qiang

Born in 1957 in Quanzhou, China. Lives and works in New York.

The work of Cai Guo-Qiang draws from both the ancient myths and aesthetic traditions of Chinese culture as well as from the work of contemporary Western science, technology and culture.

He first studied stage design in Shanghai, before leaving his native country in 1986 to pursue further study in Japan. In 1989, he first comes to public attention with *Projects for Extraterrestrials*, a series of drawings created by exploding gunpowder on Japanese paper. After 1989, the artist begins to organize ambitious and elaborate performance events using gunpowder and fireworks, setting off large explosions in the open sky. These events located in natural or urban settings are full of beauty and drama, and evoke inevitably the forces of chaos and the destructive powers of man. In 1995, Cai Guo-Qiang moves to New York where he currently resides.

Recent Exhibitions

2002

Cai Guo-Qiang: Ethereal Flowers, Galleria Civica di Arte Contemporanea, Trento

2001

Une histoire arbitraire, Musée d'art contemporain de Lyon, Lyon

2000

Cai Guo-Qiang, Fondation Cartier pour l'art contemporain, Paris

1999

I Am the Y2K Bug, Museumsquartier, Kunsthalle Wien, Vienna

1998

Day Dreaming, Cherng Piin Gallery, Taipei, Taiwan

Recent Exhibitions Catalogues and Books

Cai Guo-Qiang: Ethereal Flowers, Galleria Civica di Arte Contemporanea, Trento, 2002

Cai Guo-Qiang, Phaidon, London, 2002

Cai Guo-Qiang's APEC Fireworks Show Cannot Be Realized In Its Entirety, Chinese Art News, Taipei, 2001

Cai Guo-Qiang, Fondation Cartier pour l'art contemporain, Paris/ Thames & Hudson, London, 2000

I am the Y2K Bug, Michael Wenzel, Kunsthalle Wien/ Verlag der Buchhandlung Walther König, Cologne, 1999

Day Dreaming, Cherng Piin Gallery/The Eslite Corporation, Taipei, 1998

Cultural Melting Bath: Projects for the 20th Century, Jane Farver and Reiko Tomii, Queens Museum of Art, New York, 1997

Peter Hutton

Born in 1944 in Detroit, Michigan.
Lives and works in Annandale-on-Hudson.

Filmmaker Peter Hutton studied painting, sculpture and film at the San Francisco Art Institute. He has produced more than twenty films, most of which are portraits of cities or landscapes around the world. He uses minimal means in his approach to filmmaking, shooting black and white silent imagery with a 16 mm camera mounted on a tripod. Reminiscent of the early single-shot movies of the Lumière brothers, his films present a series of extended discrete views separated by black leaders. While the apparent lack of movement in many shots may initially evoke still photography, even the least active of Hutton's images subtly evolve, creating a mysterious and haunting effect. The serene landscapes often contain a strong undertone of environmental disturbance that confronts our desire for imagery of pristine nature.
Peter Hutton is the recipient of numerous awards including the Guggenheim fellowship and a grant from the National Endowment for the Arts. He has been the director of the Film and Electronic Arts Program at Bard College in New York since 1985. Many of his films have been shown in institutions such as the Whitney Biennial in New York, the Museum of Modern Art of New York, the Walker Art Center, Minneapolis, the New York Film Festival and the Rotterdam Film Festival.

Recent Filmography

2001-2002
Two Rivers (work in progress), 60 min

2000-2001
Looking at the Sea, 35 min

Recent Exhibitions

2002
Biennial of the Whitney Museum of American Art, New York

1995
Biennial of the Whitney Museum of American Art, New York

1990
Biennial of the Whitney Museum of American Art, New York

Recent Reviews and Articles

"The Machine in the Garden," Scott MacDonald, *Critical Cinema III*, 2001
NY Times, Stephen Holden, 2000
Critical Cinema III, Scott MacDonald, 1997

Jonas Mekas

Born in 1922 in Lithuania. Lives and works in New York.

Since the 1950s Jonas Mekas, prolific filmmaker, critic and curator, has been one of the driving forces behind New York's avant-garde film culture. He is the founder of Anthology Film Archives, the Filmakers' Cooperative and *Film Culture* Magazine. His autobiographical approach to film, which is in opposition to commercial Hollywood cinema, tends to examine the relationship between documentation and individual memory. Mekas has single handedly helped to shape the public image of avant-garde filmmaking in America.

Recent Filmography

2001
Ein Märchen aus alten Zeiten, 6 min

2000
As I Was Moving Ahead Occasionally, I Saw Brief Glimpses of Beauty, 4 hours 48 min

1999
A Few Notes on Andy's Factory, 45 min

1998
Song of Avignon, 5 min

Recent Exhibitions

2002
Documenta 11, Kassel
Musée d'Art Moderne de la Ville de Paris

1998
Le Printemps de Cahors, Cahors

1996-1997
Metropolitan Museum of Photography, Tokyo

Recent Bibliography

Lost, Lost, Lost, Pip Chodorov, Patrice Rollet, Éditions Paris Experimental, Paris, 2000
Jonas Mekas: This side of paradise, Galerie du Jour, Paris, 1999
Sustabdytos akirmikos, Contemporary Art Museum, Vilnius, 1997

Aernout Mik

Born in 1962 in Groningen. Lives and works in Amsterdam.

The videos of Aernout Mik portray groups of actors performing carefully constructed fictional scenarios. The characters in his films seem to move through space like sleepwalkers, neither communicating with each other nor reacting to interruptions from outside. Many of his works evoke the scene of some disaster, where seemingly shocked survivors occupy that liminal zone just after the tragic event but before help arrives. The absence of sound increases that dreamy feel of his work and adds to the uncertainty about what is happening.

Recent Filmography

2002

Park, video installation, 15 min, looped

Zone, 4 screen video installation, 23 min, looped

Flock, 2 screen video installation, 21 min, looped

2001

Reversal Room, 5 screen video installation, 40 min, looped

Middlemen, video installation, 21 min, looped

Glutinosity, video installation, 18 min, looped

2000

Lumber, 5 screen video installation, 18 min, looped

1999

Territorium, 2 screen video installation, 15 min, looped

Recent Exhibitions

2002

Flock, Fundació Joan Miró, Barcelona

Reversal Room, Stedelijk Museum, Bureau Amsterdam

2001

Reversal Room, The Power Plant, Toronto

Middlemen, Galerie carlier | gebauer, Berlin

Domaine de Kerghuéhennec, Bignan

2000

Small Disasters, Galerie Fons Welters, Amsterdam

3 Crowds, ICA, London

Recent Bibliography

Elastic, text by Daniel Birnbaum Heineken prize for Art 2002, 2002

Reversal Room, text by Philip Monk, The Power Plant, Toronto, 2002

Aernout Mik, primal gestures, minor roles, Stedelijk Van Abbemuseum, Eindhoven, 2000

Hanging around, Rotation, Part I: Hanging around, Museum Ludwig, Cologne, 1999

Tony Oursler

Born in 1957 in New York. Lives and works in New York.

Through the mediums of video, sculpture, computer, film and photography, Tony Oursler centers his work on the vanishing distinction between what is real and what is constructed. His work ranges from single channel videos, to video and sculpture dynamically integrated together. He is best known for his installations, confronting the spectator with a cast of strange characters projected by video. Often found in awkward places such as stuck under sofas, chairs or mattresses, the figures call out for help, complain, ramble or just look out at the spectator. Largely influenced by special effects and new technologies, Ourlser's work explores their power to imitate the emotional and spiritual capacities of man.

Recent Exhibitions

2002

Drawings, Lehmann Maupin Gallery, New York

Luftmetall, Hans Mayer Gallery, Dusseldorf

Station, Magasin 3, Stockholm Konsthall, Stockholm

2001

Antennae Pods Transmissions, Metro Pictures, New York; Institut Valencià D'Art Modern, Valencia; Galerie Ghislaine Hussenot, Paris; Galerie Joan Prats, Barcelona

2000

Sulfer, Glass, Silicon, 1000 Eventi, Milan

The Empty Cabinet, Henry Art Gallery, University of Washington, Seattle; University Art Gallery, University of California, San Diego

Tony Oursler: The Darkest Color Infinitely Amplified, Whitney Museum of American Art, New York; Lisson Gallery, London

1999

Introjection: Tony Oursler Mid-Career Survey, 1976-1999, MASS Museum of Contemporary Art, N. Adams, Massachusetts

Recent Bibliography

Station, Magasin 3, Stockholm Konsthall, Stockholm, 2002

Tony Oursler: The Influence Machine, Artangel, London, 2001

Tony Oursler, Institut Valencià D'Art Modern, Valencia, 2001

Tony Oursler: The Darkest Color Infinitely Amplified, The Whitney Museum of American Art, New York, 2000

Artavazd Achotowitch Pelechian

Born in 1938 in Leninakan, Armenia. Lives and works in Moscow.

Artavazd A. Pelechian studied cinema at the VGIK (Cinematic Institute of Moscow) in the 1960s. It was not until later in his career that his films were recognized abroad, thanks to French filmmaker Jean-Luc Godard who became his first and most ardent supporter. Today considered as one of the most important filmmakers of our time, he received the Scam Prize for Television for his whole work in 2000.
Inventor of an experimental "un-editing" technique, Pelechian threw aside the conventional rules of cinematography with his own *contrapuntal editing*. "Confronted with two important shots, the carriers of meaning, I do not try to bring them together, nor to confront them, but rather to create a distance between them..." Through this contrapuntal editing process, Pelechian creates an original circular type of film radically renewing the art of cinema.

Selected Filmography

1993
Life, 7 min

1992
End, 8 min

1982
Our Century, 50 min (1990, short version, 30 min)

1975
Seasons, 32 min

1970
Inhabitants, 10 min

1969
Us, 30 min

Selected Exhibitions/Screenings

2000
un art populaire, Fondation Cartier pour l'art contemporain, Paris

1993
Retrospective, Centre Pompidou, Paris

1992
Galerie nationale du Jeu de Paume, Paris

Selected Bibliography

Pelechian et le montage à distance, Université de Poitiers, 1998

"Un Langage d'avant Babel, Conversation entre Artavazd Pelechian et Jean-Luc Godard", *Le Monde*, April 2, 1992

"Arthur Pelechian, cinéaste d'icônes", Dominique Païni, *Art Press*, January 1992

"Pelechian, le montage-mouvement", Jean-François Pigoullié, *Cahiers du Cinéma*, n°454, 1991

Nancy Rubins

Born in Naples, Texas. Lives and works in Topanga, California.

Nancy Rubins is known for her monumental, gravity-defying, towering sculptures of airplane parts, electrical appliances or mattresses. While Rubins' assemblages are full of compositional ingenuity and beauty, her materials call to mind technological obsolescence and the discarded waste of consumer society.
After receiving her diploma in Fine Arts in 1976, Nancy Rubins discovers the extraordinary buildings of Catalan architect Antonio Gaudí as well as the fantastical bricolage work of popular artists such as Simon Rodia, who created the Watts Towers in Los Angeles. Thus inspired, Nancy Rubins begins working with found objects, creating sculptures from the detritus of consumer society. During the same period, she experiences an earthquake, an event that marks a turning point in her work. Struck by the way the concrete walls of her apartment begin to undulate, she begins to reflect upon the unstable nature of materials, experimenting in her sculptures with the principles of gravity and movement. Her monumental suspended sculptures are the direct results of these experiences.

Recent Exhibitions

2002
Mesure de Mesure, Galerie Poirel,
École Nationale Supérieure d'Art de Nancy, Nancy

2001
Summer 2001, Paul Kasmin Gallery, New York

1999
The Great Drawing Show 1550 to 1999, Kohn Turner Gallery, Los Angeles

Selected Bibliography

Mesure de Mesure, Céline Flécheux, École Nationale Supérieure d'Art, Nancy, 2002
Nancy Rubins: Sculptures, Drawings, Paul Kasmin Gallery, New York, 2001
"Nancy Rubins at Paul Kasmin," Rex Weil, *ARTnews*, 1999
Projects 49: Nancy Rubins, Sheryl Conkelton, Museum of Modern Art, New York, 1995

220

Wolfgang Staehle

Born in 1950 in Stuttgart. Lives and works in New York.

Wolfgang Staehle is widely recognized as a pioneer of the
Internet art scene. In 1991 he founded THE THING, an independent media project which became one of the seminal
online and offline forums for new media art and theory. His
most recent installation, *2001*, involves three live video feeds,
including a view of the World Trade Center. This work was
projected from September 6 to October 6, 2001 onto the walls
of Postmasters Gallery in New York. Due to the events of
September 11, the images of downtown New York took an
unforeseen and tragic dimension.
Staehle's work reflects our age of technological capability and
presents immediacy as a form of art.

Recent Exhibitions

2002

Outside the Box, University of South Florida
Contemporary Art Museum, Tampa, Florida

2001

Postmasters Gallery, New York

2000

Kunstverein Schwäbisch Hall, Schwäbisch Hall

1988

Requiem, The New Museum, New York

Moira Tierney

Born in 1969 in Dublin. Lives and works in New York.

Working in set design at a film company in Ireland sparked
Moira Tierney's interest in filmmaking. She received a Masters
degree in Fine Arts from the École nationale d'arts in Cergy-
Pontoise in 1997 and moved to New York on a Fullbright
scholarship to Anthology Film Archives in 1999. *American
Dreams #3* was shot on 16 mm from the window and roof of
her Brooklyn loft on September 11, using all of her film stock
(a combination of black & white and color negatives). Her
spontaneous and atmospheric documentary images, which
convey an intimate sensitivity, are intensified by music sounds
tracks.

Recent Filmography

2002

American Dreams #3, 5 min

2001

Radio Haiti, 4 min
American Dreams #1 & #2, 5 min
Untitled (#718), 3 min

2000

You Can't Keep A Good Snake Down, 4 min
Tiger Me Bollix, 4 min

1999

Ride City, 10 min

1998

The Sleep of Reason, 3 min
Skinflick, 3 min

Recent Exhibitions/Screenings

2002

LA Freewaves Festival, Los Angeles
Obscure Love & Death, San Francisco Art Institute
Reports from a Global Village, Ocularis, Brooklyn;
Anthology Film Archives, New York

2001

Rotterdam International Film Festival, Rotterdam
45th London Film Festival at the British Film Institute, London
8th Annual Chicago Underground Film Festival, Chicago

2000

Cinema Texas Film Festival, Austin

1999

6th Annual New York Underground Film Festival, New York

Andrei Ujica

Born in 1951 in Timisoara, Romania. Lives and works in Berlin.

With a background in literature, Andrei Ujica has published a number of stories and essays since 1968, such as *Television/Revolution Das Ultimatum des Bildes* (The Ultimatum of the Image). He has lived and worked in Germany since 1981 where he teaches literature, film and media theory. As of 1990, Ujica decides to devote himself to cinema and creates *Videogramme einer Revolution* (Videograms of a Revolution, 1992) in collaboration with Harun Faroki, which becomes a landmark film on the relationship between political power and the media in Europe in the end of Cold War Europe. His second film, *Out of the Present* (1995), tells the story of cosmonaut Sergei Krikalev, who spent ten months aboard the space station Mir, while on earth, the Soviet Union ceased to exist. *Out of the Present* has been compared to the most renowned classical films in the cinematic history such as *2001: A Space Odyssey* or *Solaris*, and is famous for being the most recognized non-fictional film of the 90's.

Lately, Andrei Ujica has also been interested in the convergence between cinematographic views and artistic scenes, thus his films became part of notorious exhibitions. For the exhibition *Unknown Quantity*, Andrei Ujica created a commission film installation on the discussion between Paul Virilio and Svetlana Alexievitch, confronting both traditions of the philosophical dialogue and the cinematograph as a "vision machine".

Recent Filmography

2002

Unknown Quantity, Geyer/Von Vietinghoff Filmproduktion Berlin, DigiBeta, 30 min

2000

2 Pasolini, Geyer/Von Vietinghoff Filmproduktion Berlin, 35mm, 12 min

Recent Exhibitions

2002

Expo 02—Exposition nationale Suisse, Arteplage Jean Nouvel, Morat

2001

el desert, Fundación "la Caixa", Barcelona and Seville

La Biennale di Venezia—Architectura, Venice

2000

le désert, Fondation Cartier pour l'art contemporain, Paris

1999

1 Monde réel, Fondation Cartier pour l'art contemporain, Paris

Unknown Quantity
A film by Andrei Ujica
with Svetlana Aleksievich and Paul Virilio

Installation: Johannes Fischer

Design: Martin Langewitz and David Caspar Schäfer, MiR Design Karlsruhe

Production team of the film *Unknown Quantity*

Director: Andrei Ujica

Assistant-director /Installation: Johannes Fischer

With Svetlana Aleksievich and Paul Virilio

Translation: Galia Ackermann and Chris Turner

Dubbing: Cathy Bernecker

Director of photography: Nico Hain

Lighting: Marc Teuscher

Sound engineers/Postsynchronisation/Sounddesign: Thomas Sauer, Volker Schmitt

Director of production: Georg Cockburn

Studio Director: Agnes Karow

Floor manager, Large Studio HfG Karlsruhe: Rolf Irmer

Stills photography: Dorcas Müller, Andreas Friedrich

Catering: Setareh Shahbazi

Image Engineer: Kai Simon

Animation: Nina Vöge

DVD–production: Institut für Bildmedien, ZKM Karlsruhe

Associate Producer: Thomas Geyer

Production Geyer/Von Vietinghoff Filmproduktion Berlin

Format: Colour DigiBeta

Duration: 30 min

With support from ZKM Karlsruhe
Institut für Musik und Akkustik/Institut für Bildmedien
and from the Hochschule für Gestaltung, Karlsruhe

Paul Virilio
Born in 1932, in Paris. Lives in La Rochelle.

Emeritus Professor at the École Spéciale d'Architecture in Paris, and chairman and director of the same institution from 1968 to 1998, Paul Virilio became editor of the *Espace Critique* collection at Editions Galilée in 1973 after the publication of his first philosophical essays.
He was awarded the Grand Prix National de la Critique in 1987.
In 1990, he became programme director at the Collège International de Philosophie, headed by Jacques Derrida, and, since 1992, has sat on the French commission concerned with housing for the poor (HCLD), chaired by Louis Besson.
Paul Virilio is an essayist with a special interest in urbanism and the strategic implications of new technologies. In addition to his numerous books, he has published widely in French and international journals. He has worked with the Fondation Cartier pour l'art contemporain on several exhibitions, the first being *La Vitesse* (1991), at Jouy-en-Josas in 1991.

Major Bibliography

Ground Zero, Verso, London, 2002

A Landscape of Events, MIT Press, London/Cambridge, Mass., 2000

The Strategy of Deception, Verso, London, 2000

The Information Bomb, Verso, London, 1999

Politics of the Very Worst, Semiotext(e), New York, 1998

Open Sky, Verso, London, 1997

The Art of the Motor, University of Minnesota Press, Minneapolis, Minnesota, 1995

Bunker Archeology, Princeton Architectural Press, New York, 1994

The Vision Machine, Indiana University Press, Bloomington, Indiana, 1994

The Aesthetics of Disappearance, Semiotext(e), New York, 1991

The Lost Dimension, Semiotext(e), New York, 1991

Popular Defense and Ecological Struggles, Semiotext(e), New York, 1990

War and Cinema—The Logistics of Perception, Verso, London, 1989

Speed and Politics, Semiotext(e), New York, 1986

Stephen Vitiello
Born in 1964 in New York. Lives in Bronxville, New York. Works in New York.

Electronic musician and sound artist Stephen Vitiello transforms incidental atmospheric noises into mesmerizing soundscapes that alter our perception of the surrounding environment. He has composed music for independent films, experimental video projects and art installations, collaborating with artists such as Nam June Paik, Tony Oursler and Dara Birnbaum. In 1999 he was awarded a studio for six months on the 91st floor of the World Trade Center's Tower One, where he recorded the cracking noises of the building swaying under the stress of the winds following Hurricane Floyd. As an installation artist, he is particularly interested in the physical aspect of sound and its potential to define the form and atmosphere of a spatial environment.

Selected Discography

2001

Bright and Dusty Things, New Albion Records

Sounds Building in the Fading Light, 10 min, vinyl, Creamgarden

2000

Fantastic Prayer, CD ROM in collaboration with Constance De Jong and Tony Oursler, Dia Center for the Arts and Prop Foundation, New York

1998

The Light of Falling Cars, JDK Productions

Solo Exhibitions

2002

The Project, New York

2001

Diapason, New York

2000

Texas Gallery, Houston

Main articles and Bibliography

"Spiritual America, From Ecstatic to Transcendent," Holland Cotter, *The New York Times*, March 8, 2002

Stephen Vitiello, Paulo Herkenhoff, Clocktower Gallery exhibition, P.S.1 Contemporary Art Center, New York, 2001

Stephen Vitiello, Greater New York, Amy Herzog, CD ROM and online catalogue, P.S.1 Contemporary Art Center, New York, 2000

"Stephen Vitiello's Art of Noises are a moveable feast," Rahma Khazam, *The Wire*, July 1999

Lebbeus Woods

Born in 1940.

Lebbeus Woods is widely regarded as the most original architectural visionary working today. His body of theoretical work have served as inspiration for architects, artists and students for over two decades.

Lebbeus Woods is most interested in zones of crisis, be they cities that have been damaged by major earthquakes or wars such as San Francisco and Sarajevo or those suffering the long-term effects of economic embargo such as Havana. Unlike a conventional architect, he deliberately picks these sites of catastrophe to build from, believing it an erasure of both history and memory to destroy the remains of existing buildings in order to mimic and rebuild what clearly did not stand up to the test of natural or human assault. Breaking down the hierarchies that shape traditional orthogonal architecture, Woods' designs consist of liberated structures made up of aggressive complex shapes and harshly organic contours which are built around existing buildings.

Recent Exhibitions

2002

Drawings, Whitney Biennial, New York

The Storm, Houghton Gallery, The Cooper Union, New York

2000

Seismicity, Intersection for the Arts, San Francisco

Lebbeus Woods: Works 1980-2000, Rosenwald-Wolf Gallery, Philadelphia

1999

Lines of Flight, Henry Urbach Gallery, New York

Recent Bibliography

Earthquake! A Post-Biblical View, Springer Edition Vienna New York, "Research Institute for Experimental Architecture Book Series," Vienna, 2001

Radical Reconstruction, Princeton Architectural Press, New York, 1997/2001

"War and Architecture 2000," *ARTBYTE*, New York, 2000

Scar, Netherlands Architecture Institute, Rotterdam, 1999

Borderline, Springer Edition Vienna New York, "Research Institute for Experimental Architecture Book Series," Vienna, 1998

The Fall by Lebbeus Woods

Associates:

Alexis Rochas

Henry Urbach

Beth Weinstein

Constructors:

Rafael Baur

Sunnie Joh

Joon Kim

Piotr Redlinski

David Ross

Dieter Vischer

And also:

Steven Holls

George Kokines

Guy Lafranchi

Mas Yendo

Acknowledgements

The Fondation Cartier pour l'art contemporain wishes to thank Paul Virilio for his enthusiasm, commitment and selfless dedication in the conception of the exhibition and the production of the catalogue.

We sincerely thank:
Svetlana Aleksievich
Dominic Angerame
Jem Cohen
Bruce Conner
Cai Guo-Qiang
Peter Hutton
Jonas Mekas
Aernout Mik
Tony Oursler
Artavazd A. Pelechian
Nancy Rubins
Wolfgang Staehle
Moira Tierney
Andrei Ujica
Stephen Vitiello
Lebbeus Woods

Together with Stéphane Maupin and Sébastien Saint Jean, who were responsible for the scenography of the exhibition

Larry Kazal, whose talents went into the design of this book

For their much-valued collaboration, we thank
L'Agence France Presse, Paris:
Bertrand Eveno, Managing Director,
Vaclav Neumann of the Magazine department
and Jean-François Le Mounier,
Director of the Photographic Department.
L'Institut National de l'Audiovisuel, Paris:
Emmanuel Hoog, Managing Director,
Anne Schuchman and Sylvie Richard of the Educational
and Cultural Development Dept.

And all who made the exhibition possible:
Cai Studio, New York: Hong Kai Wang, Jennifer Ma
Canyon Cinema Cooperative, San Francisco
Colin Cook, Los Angeles
Fei Dawei, Paris
Gagosian Gallery, New York: Sarah Watson
Galia Ackermann, Paris
Jean-Marie Perdix, New York
La Prod., Paris: Fred Praslicka, Bernard Guilite
Max Protetch, New York
Metro Pictures Gallery, New York
Modern and Contemporary Art
Los Angeles County Museum of Art, Los Angeles:
Stephanie Barron, Senior Curator
Tim Rogeberg, Los Angeles
Thomas Geyer Filmproduktion, Berlin
Ulrich Gebauer Gallery, Berlin: Marie-Blanche Carlier
Video Data Bank, New York

We would also like to thank all those who, by their advice, receptiveness and enthusiasm have, in various ways, been involved in this exhibition:

Agence Jean Nouvel, Paris: Jean Nouvel, Didier Brault

Agence Patrick Jouin, Paris

Anthology Film Archives, New York: Robert Haller

Bibliothèque nationale de France, Paris:
Sylvie Aubenas, Bernard Marbot and Anne Sanciaud

Bruce Albert, Paris

Canadian Centre for Architecture,
Megan Spriggs, "Cormier Project" Archivist

Cartier New York:
Stanislas de Quercize, Daniel Mawike, Steven Speaks

Centre Pompidou, Paris:
Jean Michel Bouhours, Curator;
Romain Lacroix, Programmer

Cinédoc, Paris: Anaïs le Gaufey, Kantuta Quiros

CNRS, Paris: Bernard Légé, researcher:
Jean-Michel Arnold, délégué général des rencontres internationales "Image et Science"

Electronic Arts Intermix, New York: Rebecca Cleman

Film Society of Lincoln Center, New York:
Graham Leggat, Director of Communication

Galara Agadjanova, Paris

Galerie Chantal Crousel, Paris:
Chantal Crousel; Nathalie Viot, Director

Imperial War Museum, London:
Jenny Wood, Curator, Department of Art

Laboratoire Sols, Solides, Structures, Institut national polytechnique de Grenoble: Professor Jacky Mazars

Jody Elff, New York

Light Cone, Paris: Christophe Bichon

Marie-Laure Bernadac, Chief Curator, Heritage

MoMA / Department of Painting and Sculpture, New York:
Robert Storr, Senior Curator;
Roxana Marcoci, Curatorial Assistant

Netherlands Architecture Institute Library, Rotterdam:
Petra van der Ree

New Museum of Contemporary Art, New York:
Dan Cameron, Director

Ocularis at Galapagos, New York: Karyn Riegel

Pedro Martinelli, São Paulo

P.S.1 Contemporary Art Center, New York:
Larissa Harris, Amy Smith and Jeffrey Uslip

Ethnies, Paris: Dominique Dauzier

Re:Voir, Paris: Pip Chodorov, President

Santa Monica Museum of Art, Santa Monica:
Clara Ennis, Associate Curator

The New American Cinema Group/
The Filmmakers' Cooperative: M. M. Serra

Walker Art Center, Minneapolis:
Philippe Vergne, Joan Rothfuss, Visual Arts Curators

Whitney Museum of American Art, New York:
Lawrence Rinder,
"Anne and Joel Ehrenkranz" Curator of Contemporary Art

We also thank the photographic agencies for their help with our research:

Bridgeman Giraudon, Paris:
Laurence Doumenc, Delphine Thibault

Cosmos, Paris: Cécile Roux

Corbis/Sygma: Paris: Françoise Carminati, Isabelle Martin

Dagli-Orti, Paris

Getty, Paris: Hervé Autran

Keystone/L'Illustration, Paris

Magnum, Paris: Sandrine Guillot, Catherine Rouvière

Max PPP, Paris

VU, Paris: Malika Barrach

Société Française de Photographie, Paris: Katia Busch

Rapho, Paris

Roger-Viollet, Paris: Delphine Desveaux

Sipa, Paris: Dominique Stephan

The Cleveland Museum of Art, Cleveland: Monica Wolf

Lastly, for transport services, we thank IAT, US Crane and Atelier 4.

With the collaboration of and

226   The exhibition *Unknown Quantity* was organized
with the support of the Fondation Cartier pour l'art contemporain under the aegis
of the Fondation de France and with the sponsorship of Cartier.

This catalogue was published on the occasion of the exhibition *Unknown Quantity*,
presented at the Fondation Cartier pour l'art contemporain in Paris,
from November 29, 2002 to March 30, 2003.

Exhibition

Director of the Fondation Cartier pour l'art contemporain: **Hervé Chandès**

Exhibition conceived by **Paul Virilio**

Curator in charge of the exhibition: **Leanne Sacramone** assisted by **Vanessa Critchell**;
with the collaboration of curators **Hélène Kelmachter** and **Grazia Quaroni**;
intern: **Céline Le Bacon**

Organisation: **Frédérique Mehdi**

Exhibition Design: **Stéphane Maupin** and **Sébastien Saint-Jean**

Fondation Cartier pour l'art contemporain

General Secretary: **Claire Livrozet**, intern: **Magali Bourcy**

Assistant to the Director: **Virginie Bergeron**, **Caroline Dahan**

Logistics Executive: **Corinne Bocquet**, intern: **Marilyne Besnier**

Press Relations: **Linda Chenit** assisted by **Nathalie Desvaux**;
intern: **Céline Bastard**

Web site/fondation.cartier.fr: **Juliette Mage**, intern: **Elisabeth de la Poype**

Bookshop, Group bookings: **Vania Merhar**

Secretariat: **Michèle Geoffroy**, **Ursula Thai**

Personnel Management: **Françoise Vagné** assisted by **Cornélia Cernéa**

General Supervisory Support: **François Romani**

Installation of the works: **Gilles Gioan**

Catalogue

Catalogue design: **Larry Kazal**, Paris

Publications: **Dorothée Charles** assisted by **Anne-Claire Boumendil**;
project assistant: **Olivier Celik**; intern: **Sophie Perceval**

Translations

Chris Turner (French-English)

Jian-Xing Too (French-English)

First published in the United Kingdom in 2003 by Thames & Hudson Ltd, 181A High Holborn, London WC1V 7QX

First published in the United States of America in paperback in 2003 by Thames & Hudson Inc., 500 Fifth Avenue, New York, New York 10110

Original French edition published by the Fondation Cartier pour l'art contemporain and Actes Sud

British Library Cataloguing-in-Publication Data

A catalogue record for this book is available from the British Library

Library of Congress Catalog Card Number 2002094859

ISBN 0-500-97625-2

Printed and bound in France by Imprimerie Le Govic, Nantes